I0752162

FRETBOARD FORENSICS SERIES ™

THE LITTLE GUITAR BOOK THAT COULD

TWELFTH POSITION

by

Walter Klosowski III

is published exclusively through:

OMNI MUSIC PRESS ®
7308 E 68th Pl Tulsa, OK 74133

http://www.omnimusicpress.com

Written, designed, edited, compiled, printed & distributed by the author.

Order Number OMP 003-012

ISBN 978-0578825649 Library of Congress Control Number: 2020925309

The Little Guitar Book That Could

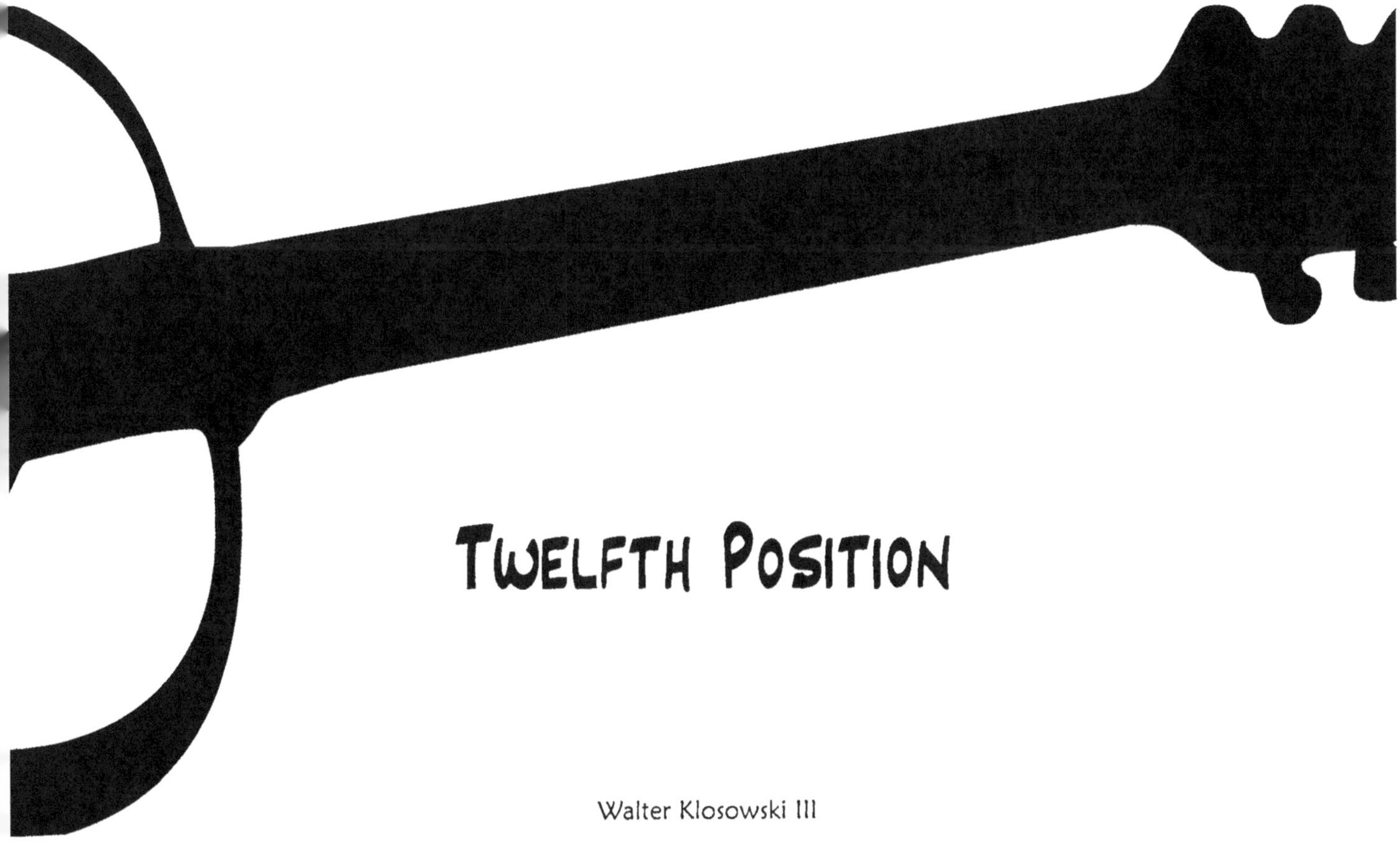

Twelfth Position

Walter Klosowski III

This book is dedicated to that astute music theorist found deep within every guitar player, or the lack thereof. As for writing it, I owe a deep personal thank you to my family who supported me and gave of their time during this project. I would also like to thank my guitar/music professors, colleagues, students and friends over the years for candidly answering my questions while sharing their unique opinions and insights.

The Little Guitar Book That Could...

... presents the C A G E D chord and scale sequence exclusively in the twelfth position for everybody to see, use and reference. This particular *Little Guitar Book That Could* does assume the following:

1) <u>Guitar position detail</u> –

There's a detailed unambiguous six consecutive fret area that delineates the twelfth position, and that position spans two octaves plus a perfect fourth...

2) <u>Fretting hand detail</u> –

The second and third fingers stay in the center of the position, generally speaking. It's the first and fourth fingers that stretch...

3) <u>Picking hand detail</u> –

This handy "(①G^{1-4} -③A^{3} -②C^{2} -②D^{1-4} -④E^{3} -⑥G^{1-4})" string picking pattern emerges when the C A G E D root note sequence is plucked alphabetically...

4) <u>MAIN ROOT NOTE DETAIL</u> –

THE **MAIN** ROOT NOTES ARE USUALLY FOUND BENEATH THE SECOND AND THIRD FINGERS. HOWEVER, HERE, ALL THREE G **MAIN** ROOT NOTE(S), AND BOTH D **MAIN** ROOT NOTE(S), FALL OUTSIDE THE EXPECTED SECOND AND THIRD FINGER REALM IN THIS, THE TWELFTH POSITION...

5) <u>OCTAVE DETAIL</u> –

THE INTERVAL BETWEEN ONE MUSICAL PITCH AND ANOTHER WITH HALF OR DOUBLE ITS OWN FREQUENCY IS AN OCTAVE. IN GUITARLAND OCTAVES ARE ROUTINELY "ONE STRING ONE FRET AWAY". HOWEVER, ON OCCASION, TWO STRINGS AND OR TWO FRETS ARE INVOLVED...

6) <u>UNISON DETAIL</u> –

WHEN TWO, OR MORE, NOTES SOUND THE IDENTICAL PITCH IT'S SAID THEY'RE IN UNISON. IN GUITARLAND IT USUALLY MEANS "SAME NOTE DIFFERENT STRING OR FRET". WHAT'S MORE, IT'S IMPLIED THE SPECIFIED UNISON OCCURS IN THE POSITION AT HAND WHEN REFERENCED...

7) <u>②ND, 2ND</u> –

SHORTHAND FOR THE ②ND STRING, 2ND FINGER <u>MAIN</u> C ROOT NOTE OR "DOT"; ANCHORING THE C MATERIAL...

8) <u>③RD, 3RD</u> –

SHORTHAND FOR THE ③RD STRING, 3RD FINGER <u>MAIN</u> A ROOT NOTE OR "DOT"; ANCHORING THE A MATERIAL...

9) <u>①ST ③RD ⑥TH, 1ST & 4TH</u> –

SHORTHAND FOR THE ①ST ③RD ⑥TH STRING(S), 1ST & 4TH FINGER(S) <u>MAIN</u> G ROOT NOTE(S) OR "DOT(S)"...

10) <u>④TH, 3RD</u> –

SHORTHAND FOR THE ④TH STRING, 3RD FINGER <u>MAIN</u> E ROOT NOTE OR "DOT"; ANCHORING THE E MATERIAL...

11) <u>②ND ④TH, 1ST & 4TH</u> –

SHORTHAND FOR THE ②ND ④TH STRING(S), 1ST & 4TH FINGER(S) <u>MAIN</u> D ROOT NOTE(S) OR "DOT(S)"...

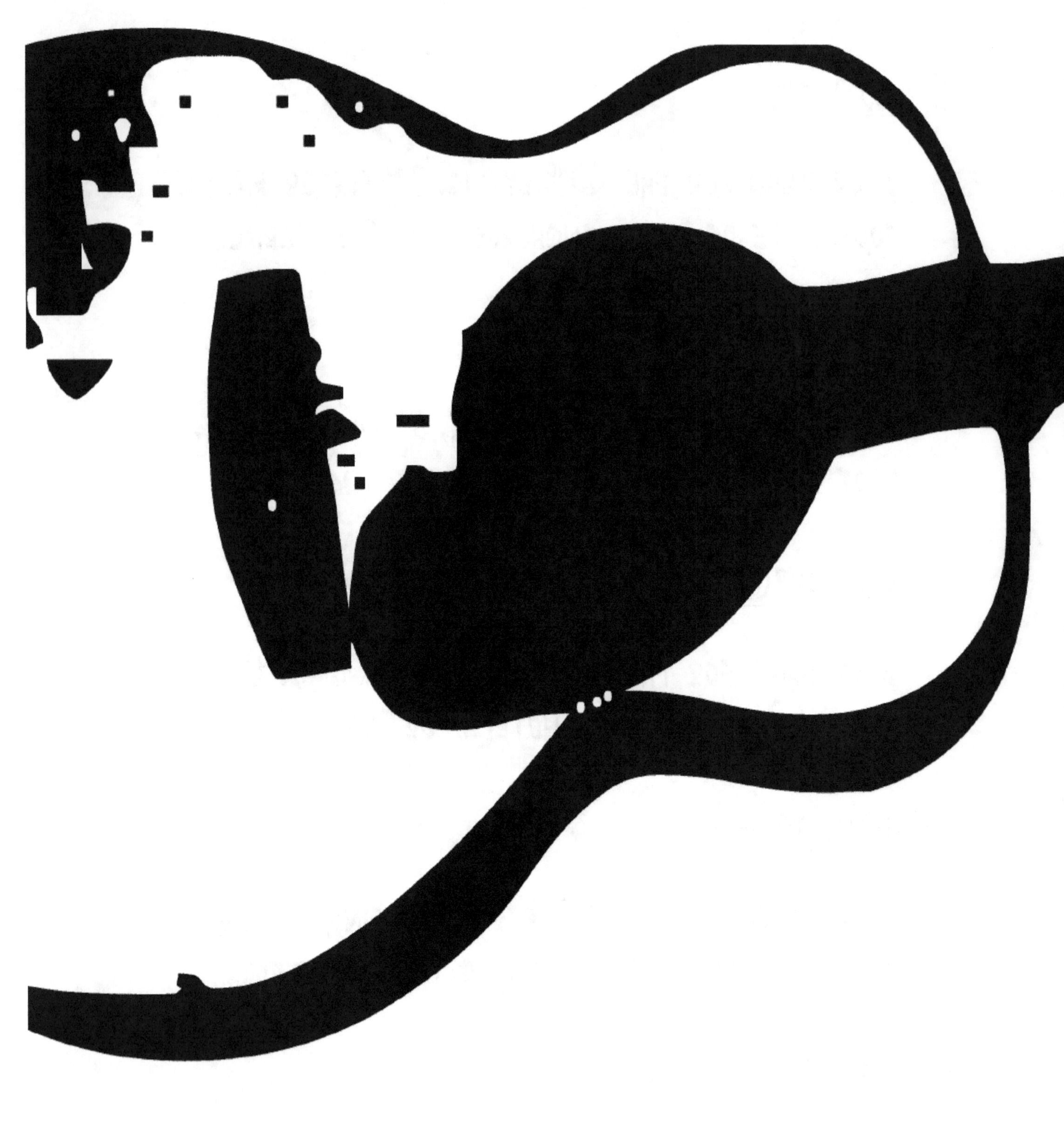

Table of Contents

Table of Contents ...

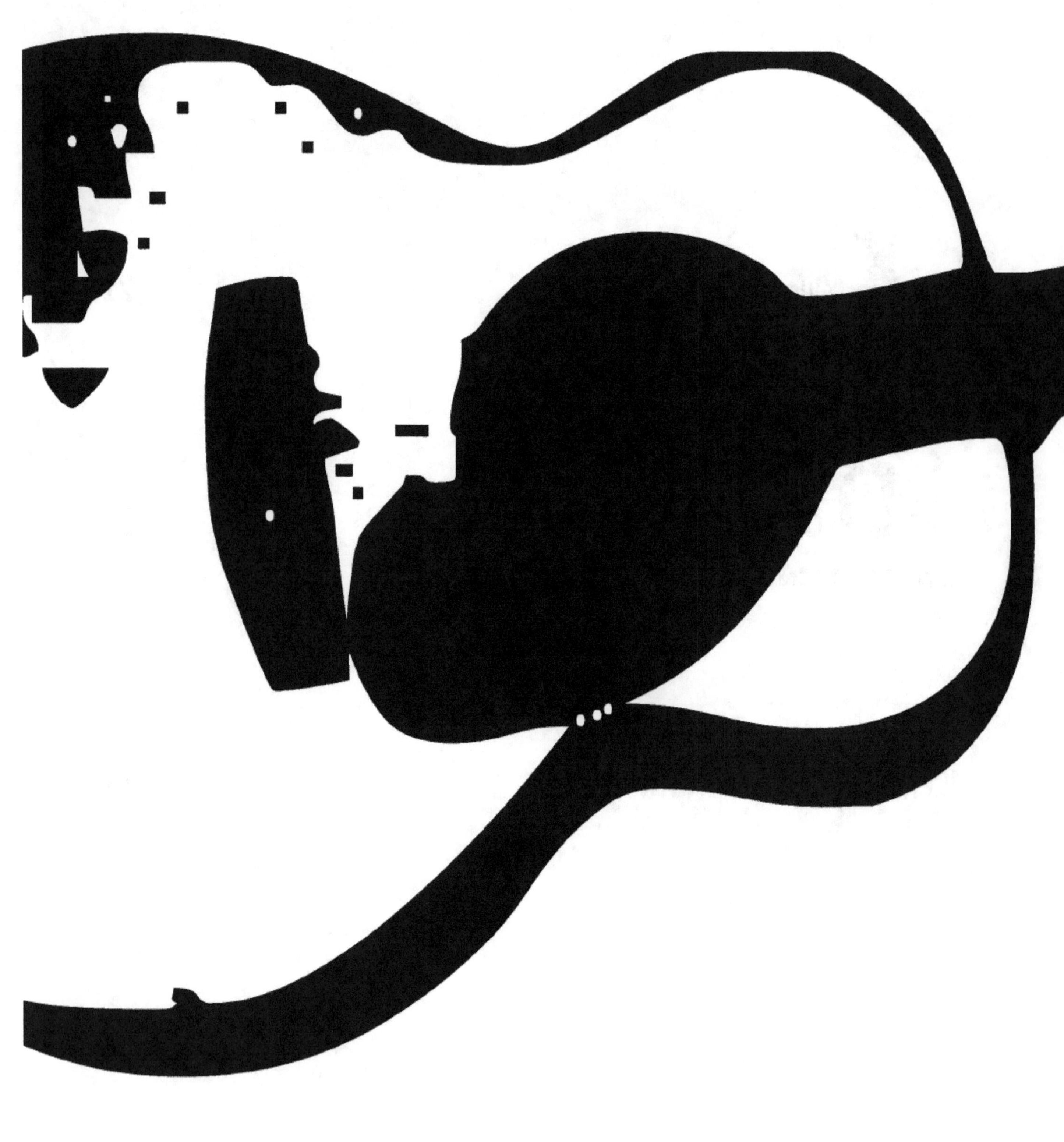

Twelfth Position Preface

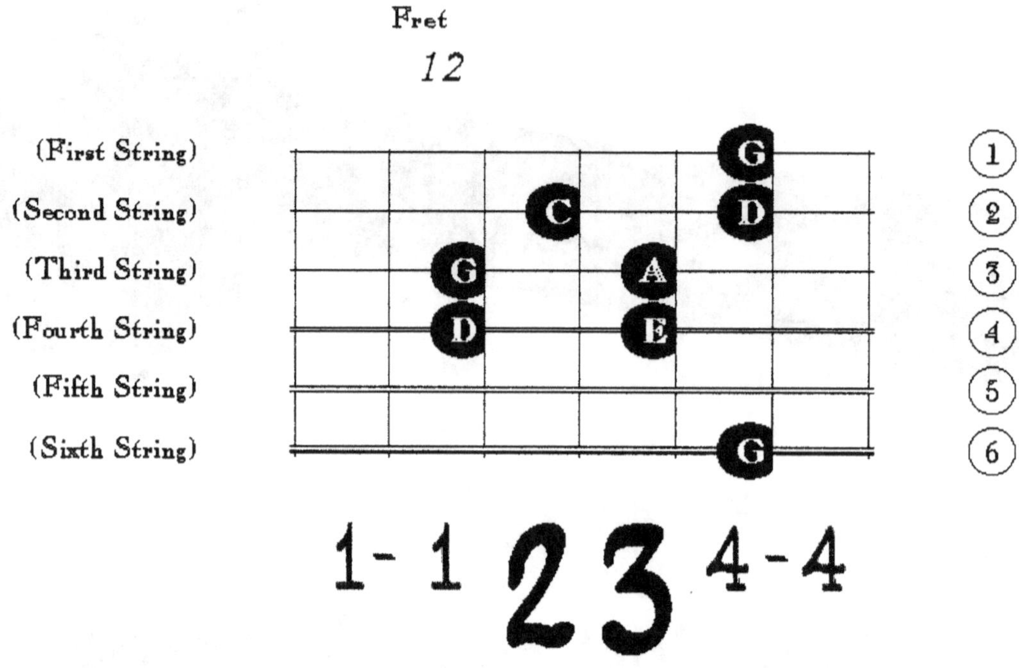

THIS GRID DETAILS THE COLLECTIVE MAIN ROOT NOTES INVOLVED WITH THE TWELFTH POSITION'S C A G E D CHORD AND SCALE SEQUENCE. NOTICE THE FIRST OR THINNEST STRING IS ON TOP, AND IT HAS SIX CONSECUTIVE FRETS, VERY IMPORTANT. THAT SAID, THE FINGERS CENTER THEMSELVES INSIDE THE SIX FRETS, ONE FINGER PER FRET, LEAVING THE OUTERMOST FRETS EMPTY. THE SECOND AND THIRD FINGERS DO REMAIN IN THE CENTER OF THE POSITION, MOST OF THE TIME, AS THE FIRST AND OR FOURTH FINGERS STRETCH. MOREOVER, THE ROOT NOTES FOUND CLUSTERING BENEATH THE SECOND AND THIRD FINGERS ARE CALLED MAIN ROOT NOTES, AND THEY INVOLVE THOSE PARTICULAR BEFORE

MENTIONED FINGERS. BUT, THERE ARE EXCEPTIONS, AND IN THIS POSITION, NO DOUBT, THE G AND D **MAIN** ROOT NOTES ARE SUCH, THEY USING THE FIRST AND OR FOURTH FINGERS. NONETHELESS OBSERVE THE FINGERING EXAMPLE BELOW FOR FURTHER CLARIFICATION.

TWELFTH GUITAR POSITION, FINGERING DETAIL, COMPLETE WITH STRETCHES

12TH FRET

1-1 2 3 4-4

POSITION NUMBER BEHIND SECOND FINGER, ONE FINGER PER FRET [1]

IN GUITARLAND THE FIRST FINGER IS DEPENDABLE AND DOES DWELL IN ITS FRET A GOOD DEAL OF THE TIME; TRUE. BUT THE FIRST FINGER OFTEN DOES, AND MAY ALSO, STRETCH A FRET. DUE TO THIS ATTRIBUTE, ONE MUST THEN FURTHER SURMISE THAT IT'S THE FRET NUMBER IMMEDIATELY BEHIND THE SECOND FINGER, AND NOT THE FIRST FINGER IN AND OF ITSELF, THAT DETERMINES LOCALE. THE SECOND AND THIRD FINGERS DO, IN GENERAL, OCCUPY THE CENTER FRETS WITH NO SPACE, NOR A STRETCH. THE FIRST AND FOURTH FINGER AREAS OCCUPY THE OUTER FRETS, AND FOLLOW THE CENTER FRET MATERIAL IN THE LEARNING. AND LAST, THIS POSITION SPANS A COMPLETE MUSICAL TWO OCTAVES PLUS A PERFECT FOURTH, IN THE GUITAR'S STANDARD TUNING.

[1] MICK GOODRICK, *THE ADVANCING GUITARIST, APPLYING GUITAR CONCEPTS & TECHNIQUES*, MILWAUKEE, WI. HAL LEONARD MUSIC PUBLISHING, 1987, PAGES 27-29

THESE ARE THE FOUR CHORD TYPES PRESENTED IN THIS BOOK. THE ROWS PROVIDE ALTERNATE VOICING CHOICE.

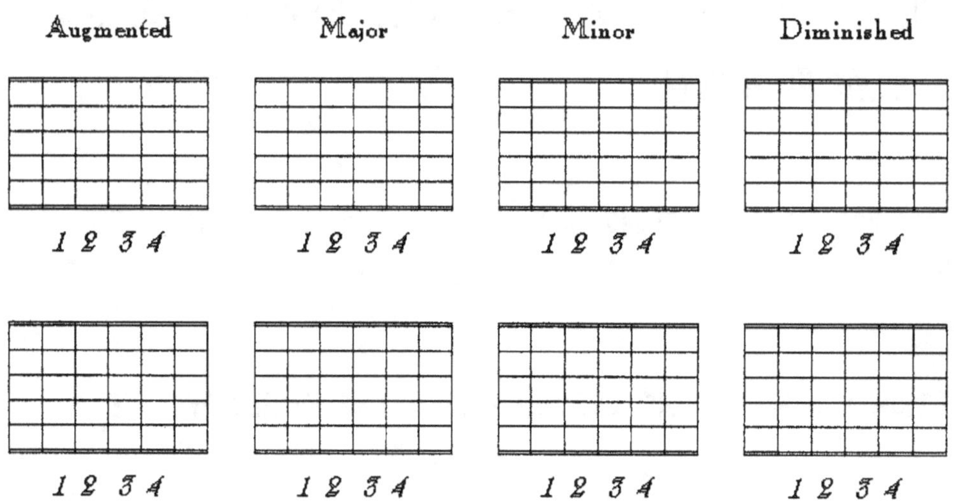

DO UNDERSTAND THAT THE CHORD SEQUENCE PRESENTED IS DELIBERATE SUCH THAT AS THE EYES TRAVERSE THE IMAGES FROM LEFT TO RIGHT, OR VISE VERSA, ONLY ONE NOTE WILL BE ALTERED OR CHANGED. OBSERVE THE AUGMENTED CHORD BEGINS AS IT MORPHS OVER TO MAJOR, THE FIFTH IN FLUX. AS THE MAJOR CHORD FOLLOWS, IT THEN MORPHS TO MINOR WITH THE ALTERED THIRD. IT ENDS WITH THE MINOR CHORD MORPHING OVER TO THE DIMINISHED VIA THE ALTERED FIFTH. PLACING THE CHORD MATERIAL IN THIS LIGHT LEAVES LITTLE TO CHANCE ENHANCING ITS MEMORIZATION. THE GRIDS ATOP THE PAGE DETAIL THE CHORD TYPE; ANY RELATED MATERIAL, LIKE THE DOMINANT SEVENTH, IS PLACED BENEATH.

Augmented chord – (brings musical tension)

This chord type consists of one major third interval with yet another major third interval placed on top. From the root, it's a major third with an augmented fifth. The dominant seventh brings tension as well.

Major chord – (brings musical stability)

This chord type consists of one major third interval with one minor third interval stacked on top. From the root, it's a major third interval; but now with a perfect fifth.

Minor chord – (brings musical stability)

This chord type consists of one minor third interval with one major third interval stacked on top. From the root, it's a minor third interval with the familiar perfect fifth as is.

Diminished chord – (brings musical tension)

This unavoidable chord type consists of a minor third interval with another minor third interval stacked on top. Given, it's a minor third with a diminished fifth.

These are the four scale types presented in this book. The rows provide alternate voicing choice.

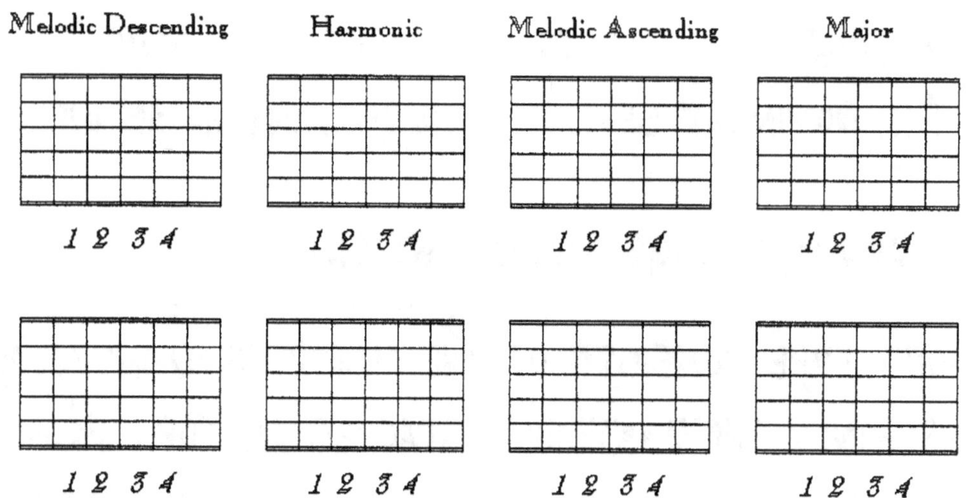

When the eyes traverse the scales left to right, or otherwise, only one note will be altered or changed. Look to see; as the melodic minor descending morphs to the harmonic, only the seventh scale degree will change. From there, as the harmonic minor morphs to the melodic minor ascending (or jazz minor) only the sixth scale degree will change. Last, as the melodic minor ascending morphs to the major scale, only the third scale degree will change. Deliberately putting the material in this light simplifies its learning. The grid row atop details the scale; any related material such as the minor pentatonic is placed beneath.

Melodic minor scale descending form

This scale variety is identical to the aeolian, natural or pure minor. The minor pentatonic scale is likewise derived from it. The very useful "three on a string" minor pentatonic is placed beneath the melodic minor.

Harmonic minor scale

This scale type is the traditional minor scale taught in the various music textbooks, scholarly references and methods. It is usually presented as opposite to that of the more blissful sounding major scale.

Melodic minor scale ascending form

This scale type is also recognized as the jazz minor scale. It is typically presented as corresponding to the descending melodic minor previously discussed.

Major scale

This scale type is most significant. All of the major keys, all of the minor keys, and all of the modes are based on it. It's routinely used when demonstrating and or conveying other musical criteria as well.

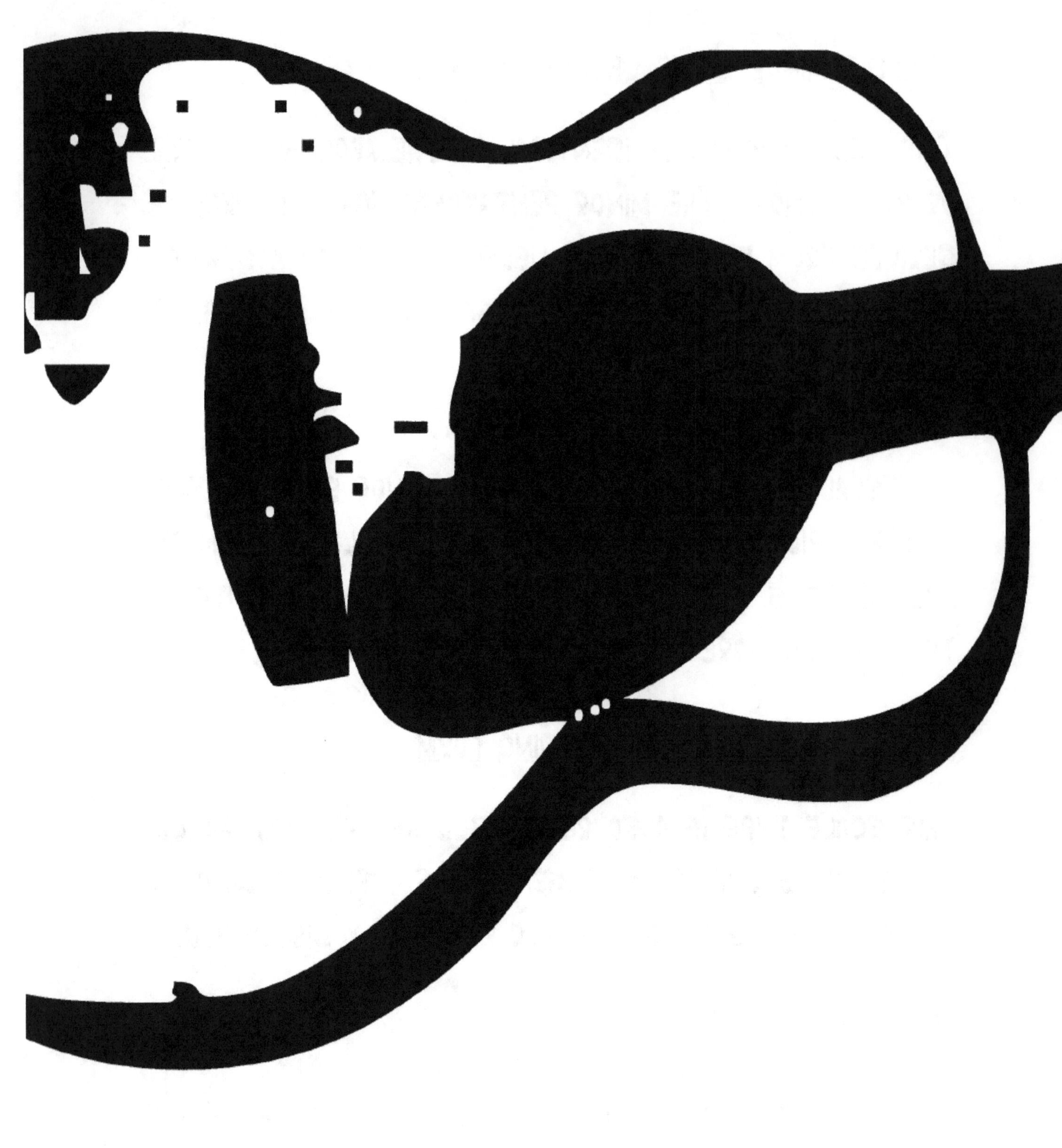

Twelfth Position

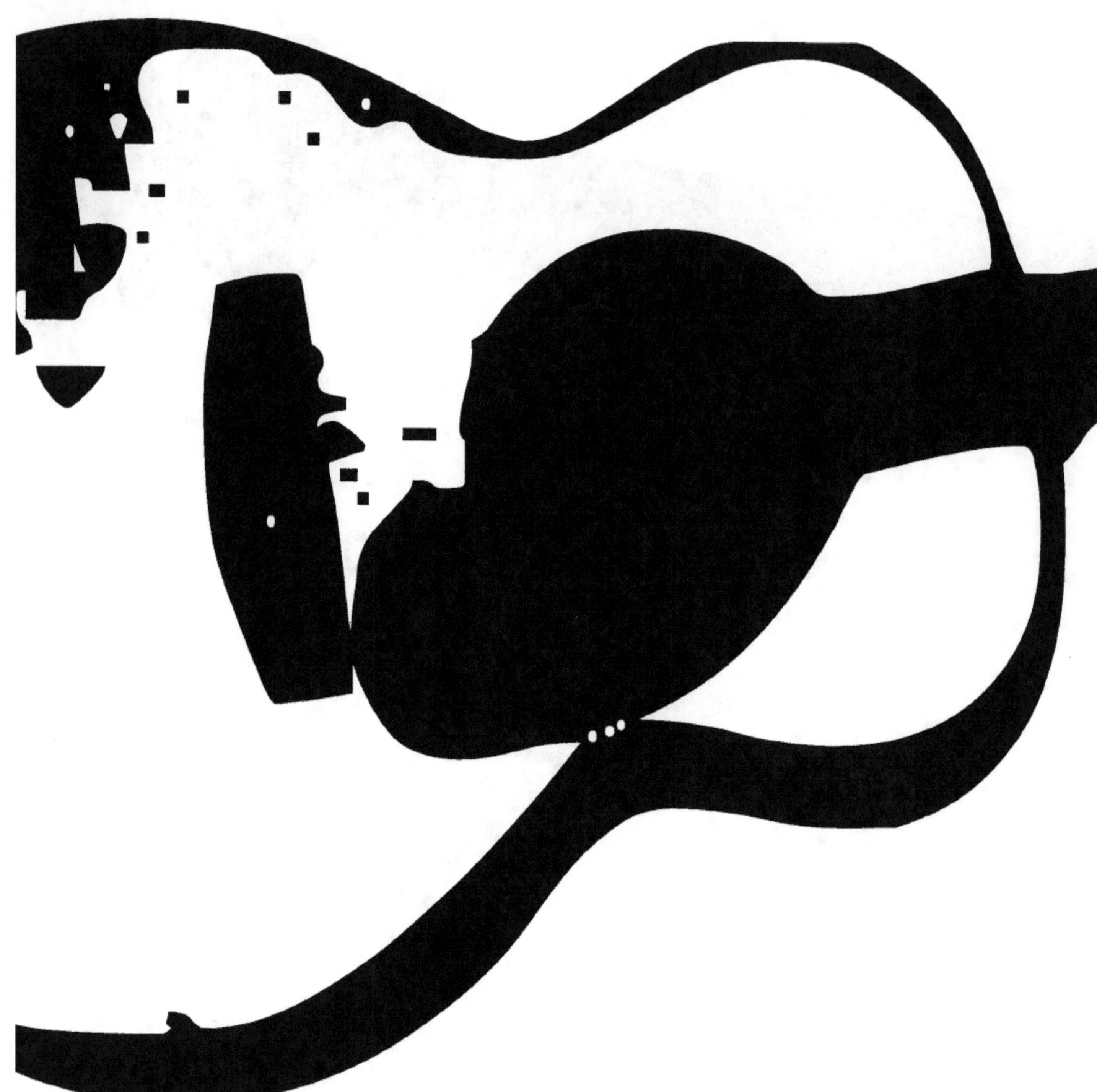

THE C CHORDS AND SCALES

OR

"THE ②ND STRING, 2ND FINGER SHAPES"

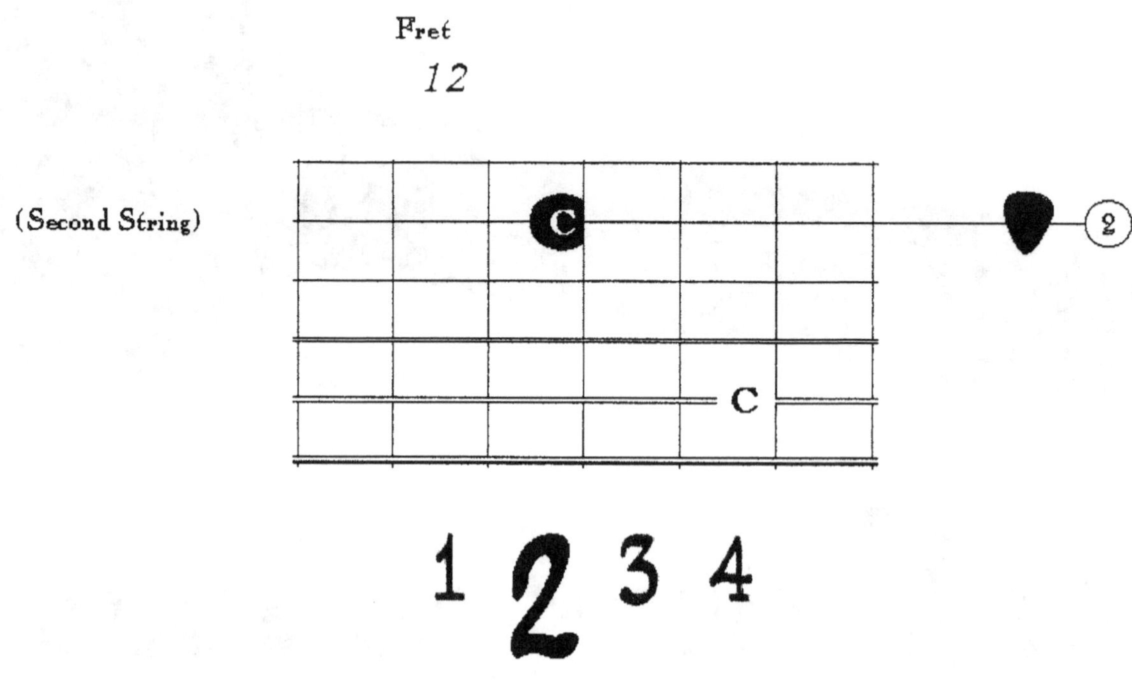

THE ROUSING "SECOND STRING SECOND FINGER" SHAPE CONSTRUCT UNDERSCORES ALL THE C CHORDS AND SCALES IN THIS POSITION. THE MAIN C ROOT NOTE IS FIXED ON THE SECOND STRING UNDER THE SECOND OR MIDDLE FINGER, THAT FINGER FRETTING. THE "DOT" PROVIDES AS AN ANCHOR POINT HELPING GROUND THE IMPLICATED FINGER WORK. THE OTHER C ON THE FIFTH STRING IS A PERFECT OCTAVE FROM THE MAIN C ROOT NOTE, AND THE PINKY FRETS IT; IF BY DESIGN. ☞

Some of the C chord voicings associated with the guitar's twelfth position are:

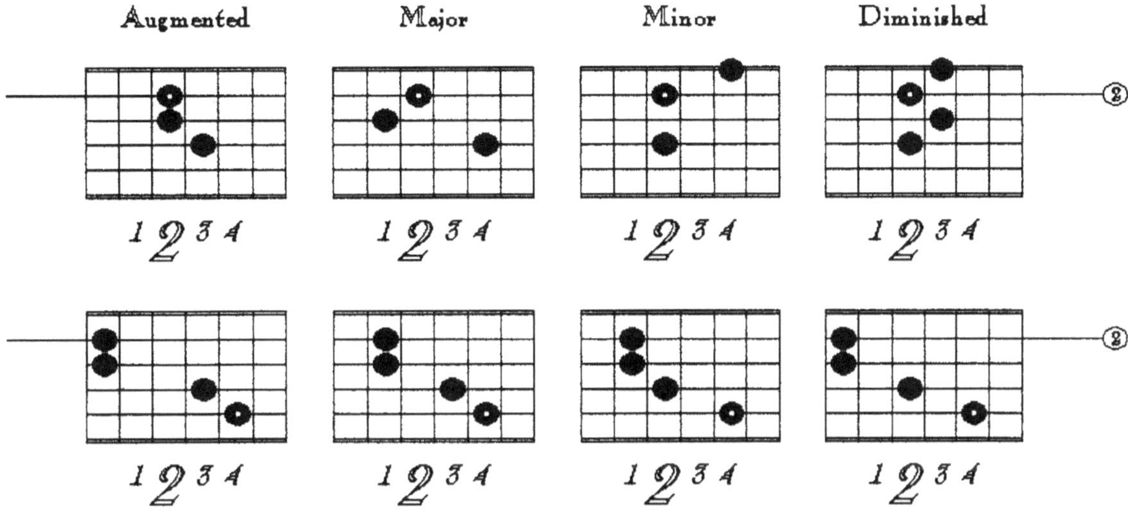

Some of the C scale voicings associated with the guitar's twelfth position are:

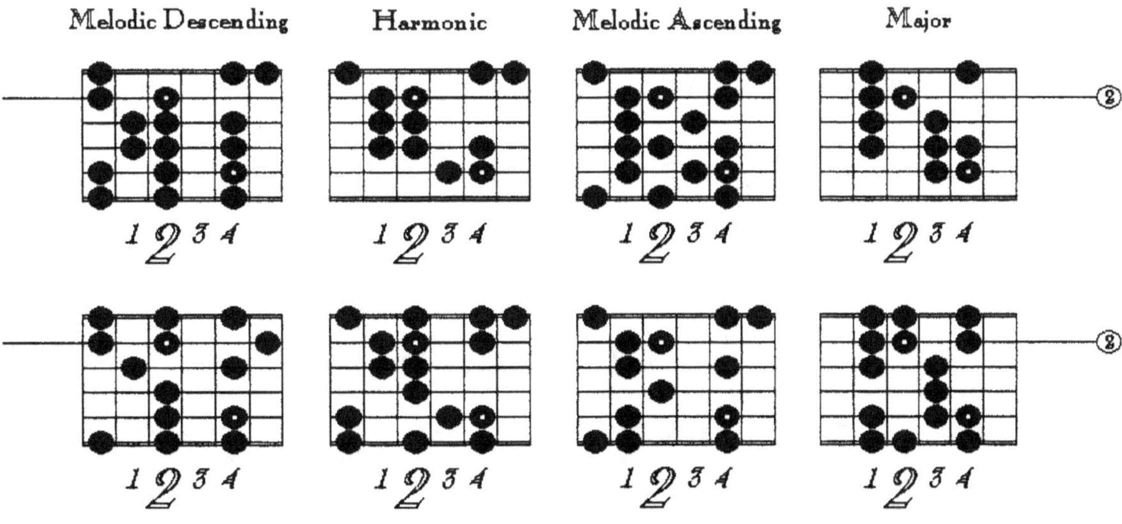

Further Commentary...

All the C chords and scales fit together great in this position, much like puzzle pieces do, and each subsequent form or pattern from here can function in any other position too. Notice also the C chords tend to utilize the treble set of strings a good deal of the time. It's somewhat subtle, but true. As for the scales, it's going to be the inside set of strings that gets used most, no thick or thin E, where the lonely full octave is. Do become aware of both situational tendencies, and musically compensate. Also, it should be mentioned that this position is prone to open string use, being an upper position, as the present chords and scales can profit from such use. Often open strings are the solution to cumbersome fingering situations as well.

THAT ASIDE, LOOK HOW THE LOWER OCTAVE C ON THE FIFTH STRING IS PAIRED WITH THE MAIN C ROOT NOTE IN THE GRIDS. THE PINKY FINGER FRETS IT, COMMON SENSE DICTATING NO OTHER CHOICE. IT REQUIRES NO STRETCH, MAKING ANY TECHNICAL NECESSITIES MUCH LESS ARDUOUS.

BOTH C'S DISCUSSED IN THIS SECTION ARE EQUAL IN TERMS OF MUSICAL PURPOSE. BUT THERE'S NO NEED TO CONSTANTLY VOICE BOTH OF THEM ALL THE TIME, OR BOTH AT THE SAME TIME, IN EVERY C CHORD AND SCALE PLAYED.

The A Chords and Scales

or

"The ③rd String, 3rd Finger Shapes"

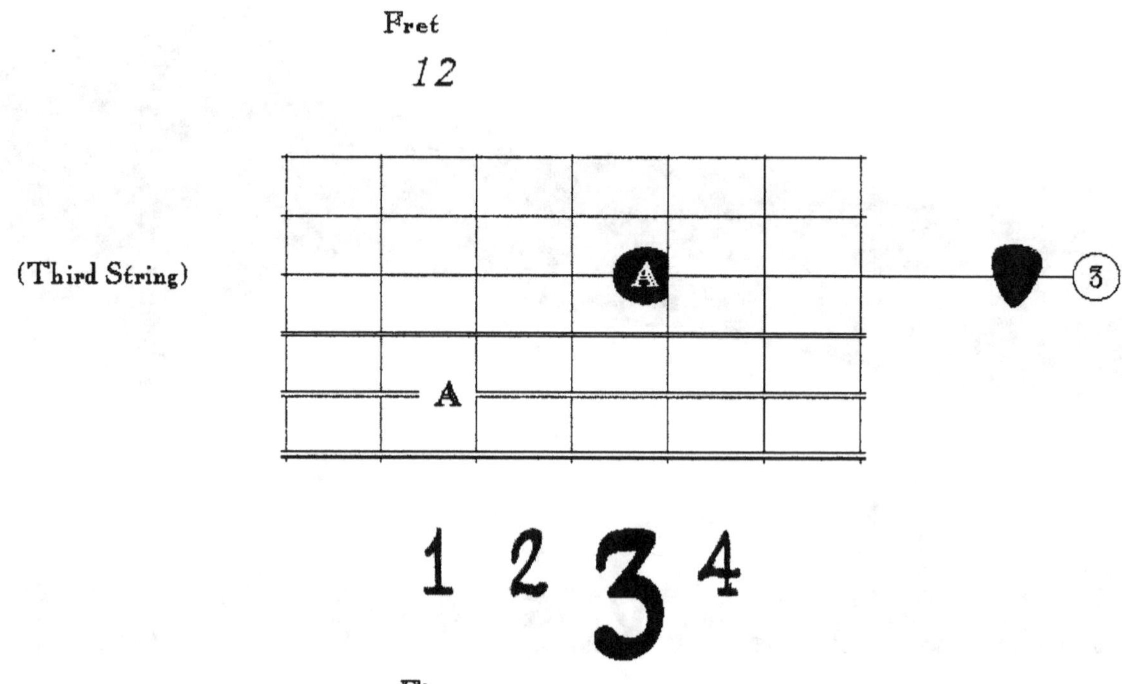

THE ABOVE "THIRD STRING THIRD FINGER" SHAPE CONSTRUCT UNDERSCORES ALL A CHORDS AND SCALES IN THE TWELFTH POSITION. BOTH A'S ARE AN OCTAVE APART FROM EACH OTHER, THE MAIN A ROOT NOTE BEING ON THE THIRD STRING, THE THIRD FINGER FRETTING. THE OTHER A IS, UNSURPRISINGLY, FRETTED WITH THE INDEX FINGER, AND FOR APPARENT REASONS. THE "DOT" CONVEYS STABILITY AND HELPS ORIENTATE THE FINGERING CONCERNED WHEN PLAYING THIS A MATERIAL. ☞

Some of the A chord voicings associated with the guitar's twelfth position are:

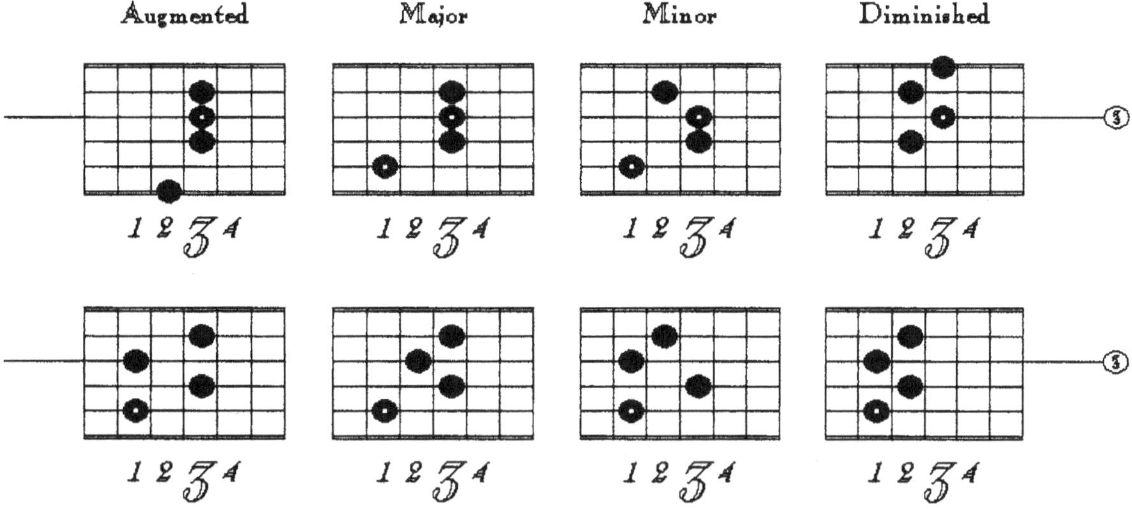

Some of the A scale voicings associated with the guitar's twelfth position are:

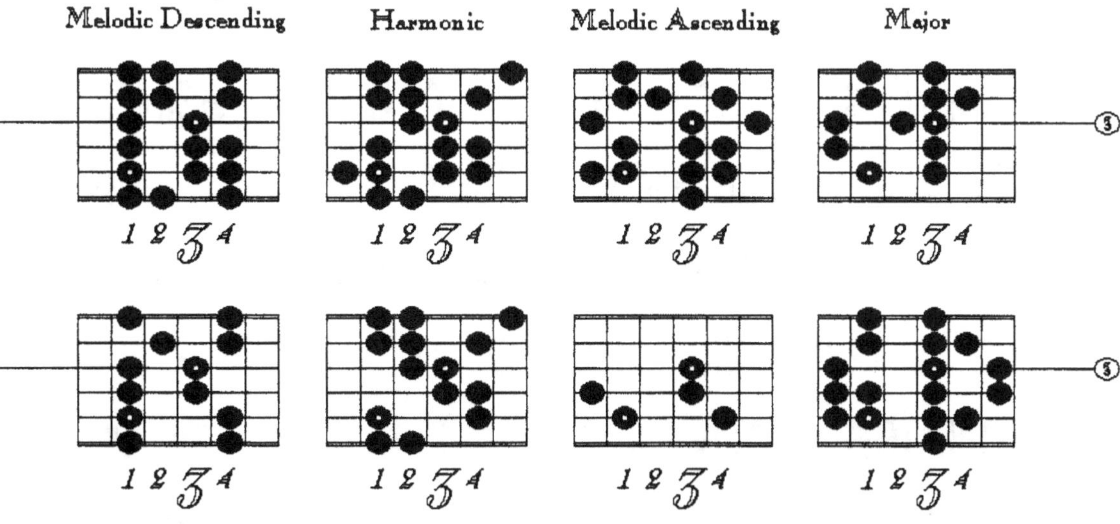

Further Commentary...

All the A chords and scales collectively fit in the twelfth position framework like pieces of a puzzle, and its subsequent forms and patterns can likewise function in any other position too, mind the slight fingering changes if any. When playing this material, notice the third and first fingers work together best, and know that the lower octave A on the fifth string is virtually the only other A that can be voiced along with the **main** A root note. That said, the open fifth A string is a great musical option, it being two octaves below the **main** A root note in question or one octave below the remaining A. And know guitarists regularly include it. There's also a technical issue surrounding the third finger on the fretting hand that occurs when voicing the

A major chord. The third or ring finger is very significant to the chord, in that it has options. It can, and often does, barre three out of the four strings involved, or the remaining middle and pinky fingers can join the third finger to assist. Obviously, the fret space is narrow in this position, but some players will delicately manage to negotiate all three fingers into the space. But as always, the melodic line is what truthfully governs the fingering choices.

The A's as discussed in this text are musically equal. However, don't voice both of them every time or all the time, or both simultaneously, in every A chord or scale played.

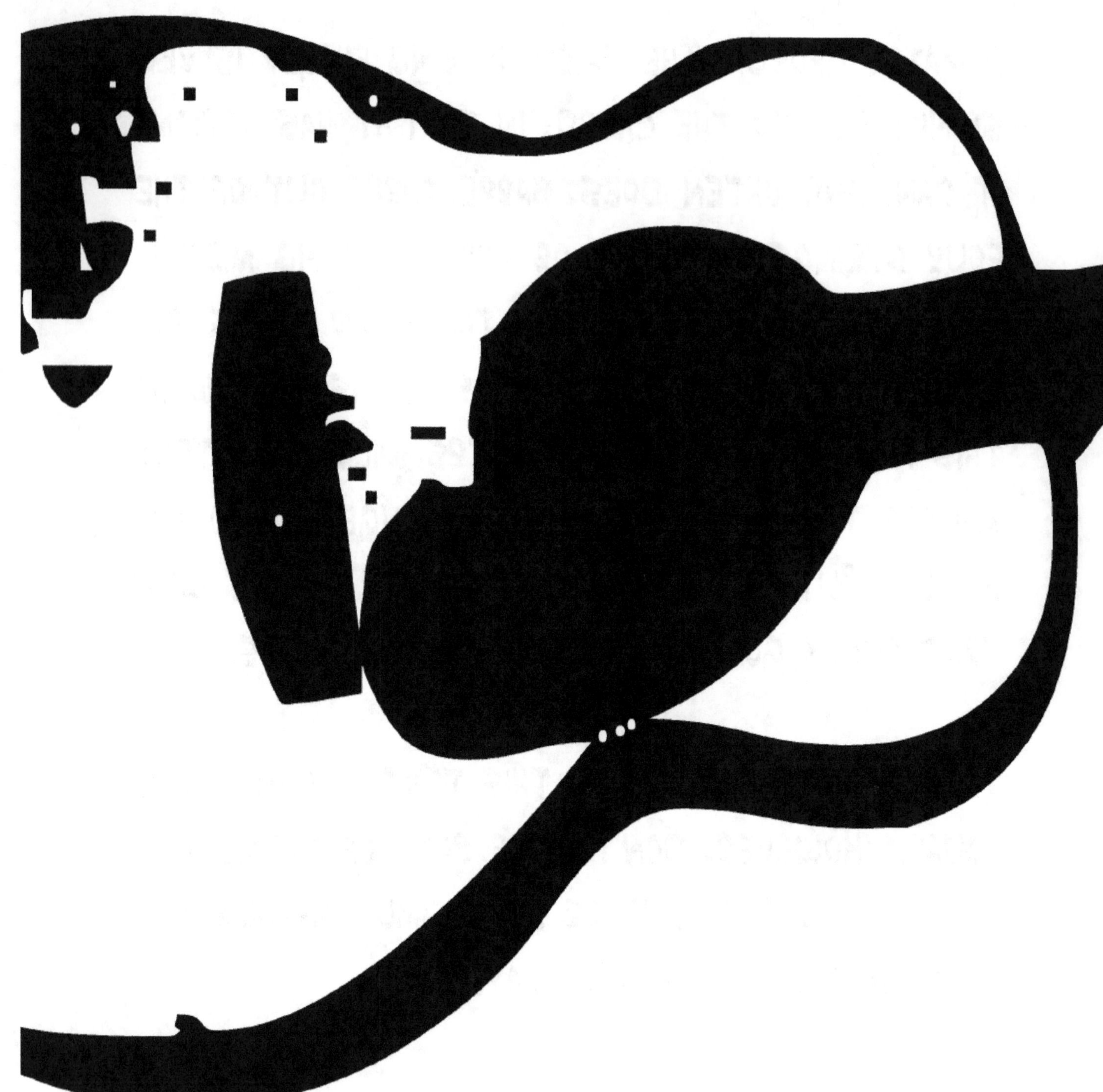

The G Chords and Scales

or

"The ①st / ③rd / ⑥th String(s), 1st & 4th Finger(s) Shapes"

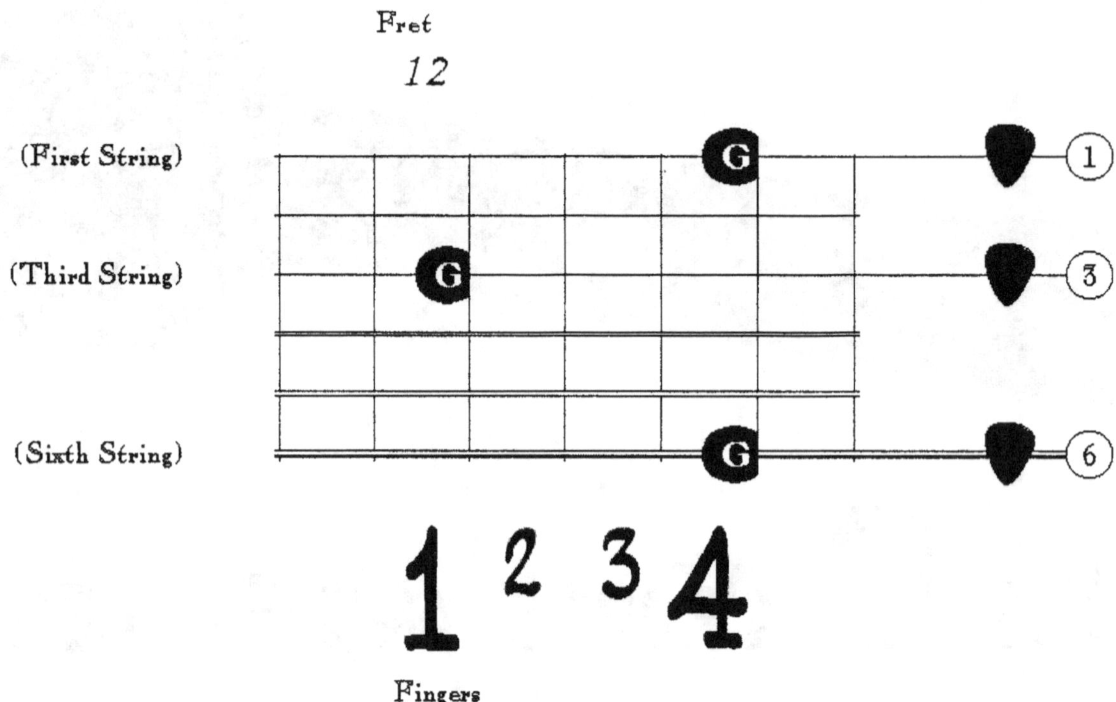

THIS SHAPE CONSTRUCT UNDERSCORES EACH G CHORD AND SCALE IN THE TWELFTH POSITION. THE MAIN G ROOT NOTE(S) ARE FIXED ON THE FIRST / THIRD / SIXTH STRING(S) AND ARE FRETTED WITH THE FIRST AND OR FOURTH FINGER(S); NOT THE USUAL SECOND AND THIRD. THIS IMPARTS SOME ODD TECHNICAL TRAITS TO THE MATERIAL, AS SEEN IN THE GRIDS. THE "DOT(S)" ASSIST WITH ALL FINGER WORK CONFIGURATION, BUT NOT ALL THREE NEED BE VOICED SIMULTANEOUSLY. ☞

Some of the G chord voicings associated with the guitar's twelfth position are:

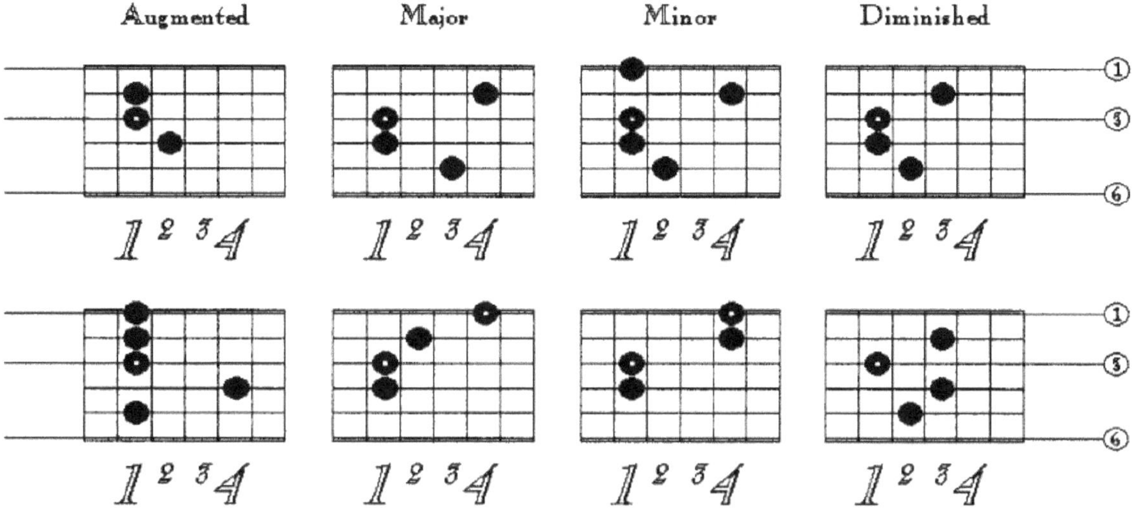

Some of the G scale voicings associated with the guitar's twelfth position are:

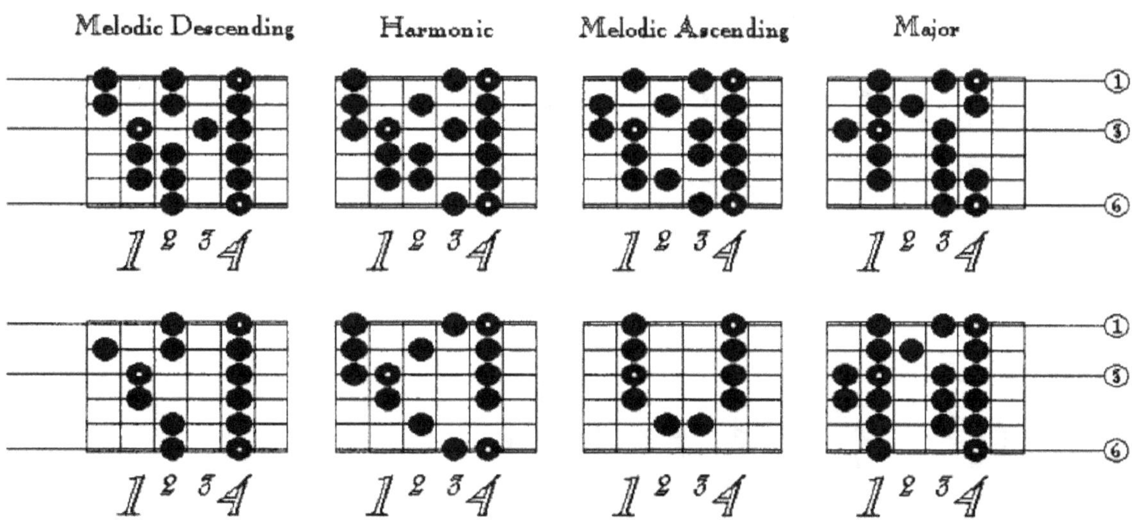

Further Commentary...

All the G chords and scales fit in the twelfth position framework as puzzle pieces do, and all its ensuing forms and patterns work just fine in other positions as well. The "dot(s)" in the grids help with visualizing the finger work and such, but they also impart a sense of technical feel all their own, being that the first and or fourth fingers are used instead of the second and third. Notice, the first finger coordinates with the fourth quite a bit when playing this G material, both fingers also barring a lot of the time. Such technique is quite obvious when the fourth finger deals with the G on the thinnest string during a potential double stop or power five. Also, guitarists are sure to take musical advantage of the open third G string, as it's a

PERFECT OCTAVE AWAY FROM THE **MAIN** G ROOT NOTE ON THE SAME STRING IN THIS UPPER POSITION. AND LAST, AFTER USING THIS CONSTRUCT REGULARLY, IT BECOMES APPARENT THAT CERTAIN TECHNICAL ISSUES RELATED TO GUITAR POSITIONWORK ARE MORE READILY UNDERSTOOD HERE. THIS IS BECAUSE ALL THREE G'S ARE **MAIN** ROOT NOTE(S), THAT'S THE LOWER, MIDDLE AND UPPER, PLUS THERE'S NOT MUCH STRETCHING TO BE HAD OF THE FINGERS IN THE HIGHEST OCTAVE.

TO CLOSE, ALL G'S DISCUSSED IN THIS SECTION ARE MUSICALLY EQUAL. BUT THERE IS NO NEED TO VOICE ALL THREE EVERY TIME, OR ALL SIMULTANEOUSLY, IN THE G CHORDS AND SCALES PLAYED.

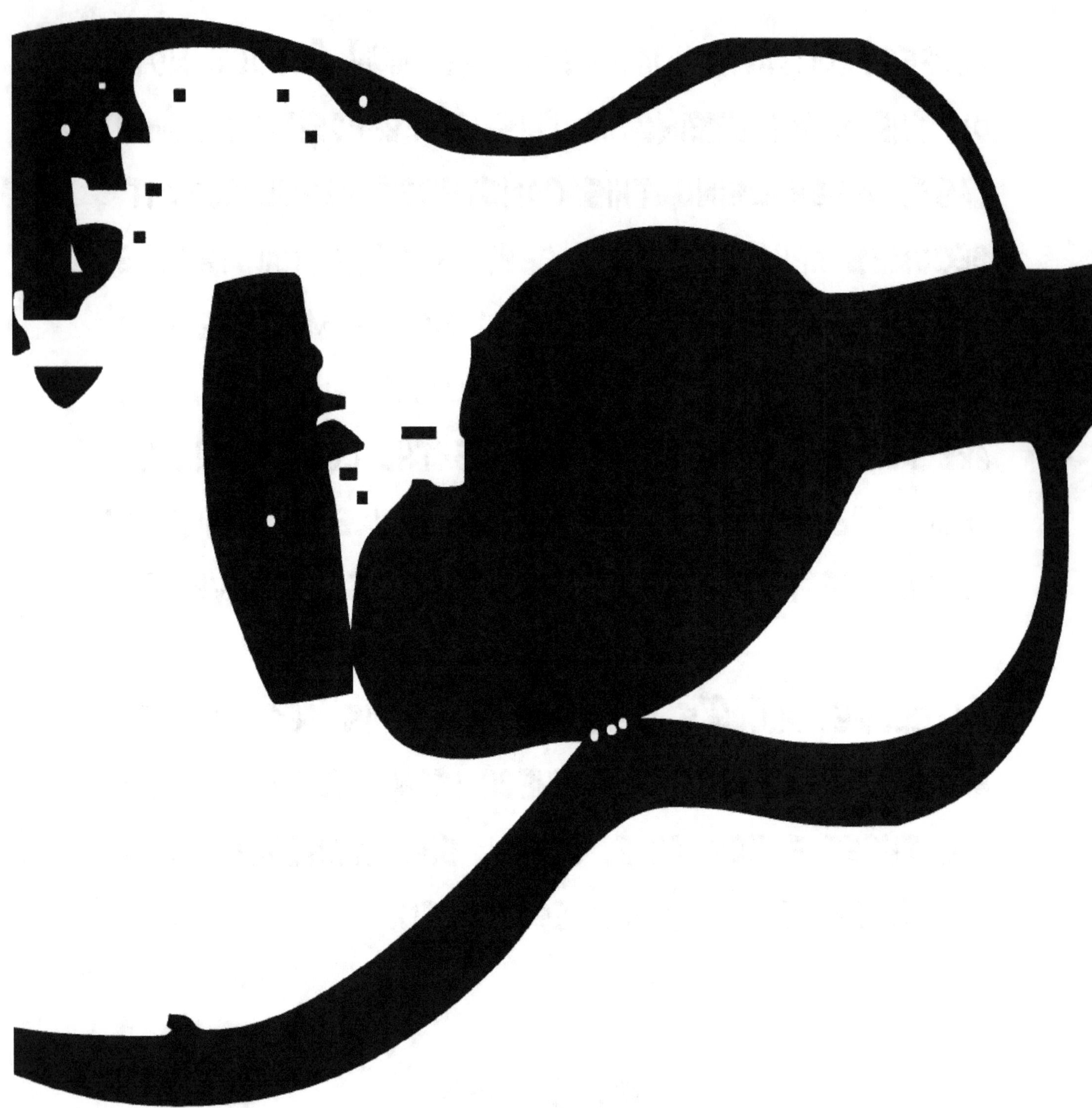

THE E CHORDS AND SCALES

OR

"THE ④TH STRING, 3RD FINGER SHAPES"

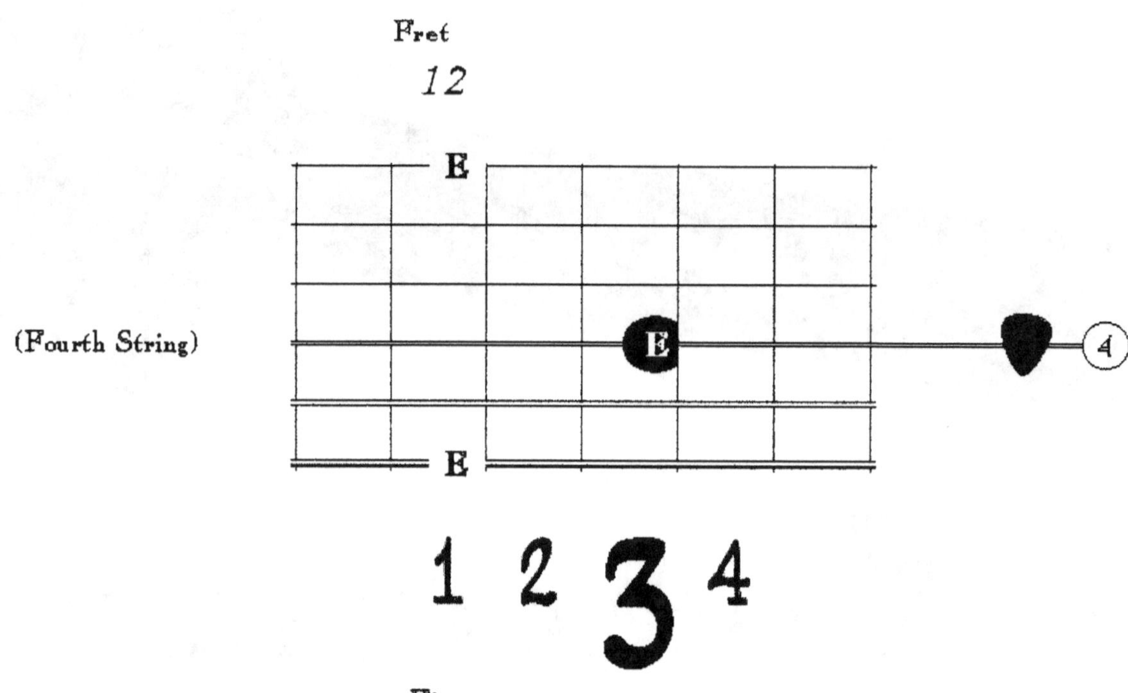

THE RESPECTED "FOURTH STRING THIRD FINGER" SHAPE CONSTRUCT UNDERSCORES ALL THE E CHORDS AND SCALES IN THIS POSITION. THE <u>MAIN</u> E ROOT NOTE IS FIXED ON THE FOURTH STRING BENEATH THE THIRD FINGER, THAT PARTICULAR FINGER FRETTING. THE INDEX FINGER, BARRED OR BOORISHLY, FRETS THE OTHER PAIR OF E'S ON THE FIRST AND OR SIXTH STRINGS AN OCTAVE AWAY. IT APPEARS QUITE OBVIOUS THAT THE THIRD AND FIRST FINGERS MANAGE THE TECHNIQUE WHEN PLAYING THIS MATERIAL. ☞

Some of the E chord voicings associated with the guitar's twelfth position are:

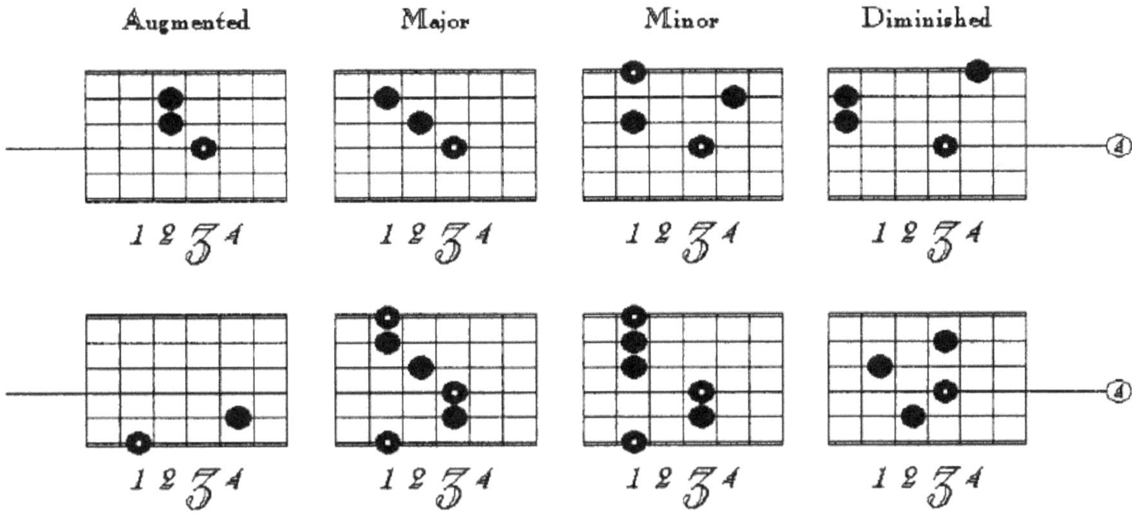

Some of the E scale voicings associated with the guitar's twelfth position are:

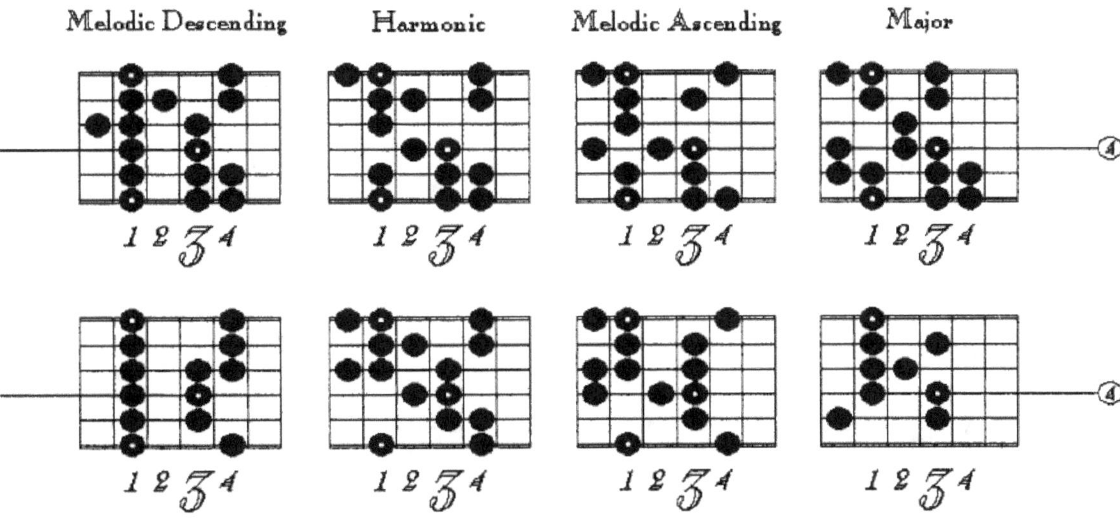

Further Commentary...

All the E chords and scales fit in the twelfth position framework so neatly and, perhaps with some slight fingering adjustment, each ensuing form and pattern can function just fine in any other position as well. It's important to know that, over time, these shapes and patterns have become very popular indeed, none more so than the minor pentatonic scale as it's portrayed in the various guitar method books and videos. It is unquestionably one of the preferred musical vessels, and some guitarists might even argue that it's depended upon too much. Even so, it remains practical to fully vet all E chord and scale material in the twelfth position early on, prior to moving its ensuing forms and patterns about the neck.

ALSO WHEN FRETTING THESE E CHORDS AND SCALES, NOTICE THE SUBTLE WAY IN WHICH THE THIRD FINGER MAINTAINS ITS PRIORITY IN THE FINGER WORK. THIS IS DUE TO THE PRESENCE OF THE MAIN E ROOT NOTE BEING LOCATED UNDER IT, MOSTLY. AND, AS A SORT OF TECHNICAL BONUS, THERE IS LITTLE IF ANY FINGER STRETCHING AMONGST THE OTHER E OCTAVES, LOWER OR HIGHER. IN CONCLUSION, REMEMBER TO TAKE FULL ADVANTAGE OF THE OPEN STRINGS, THE FIRST OR THE SIXTH E'S IN PARTICULAR, AS THOSE ARE ONE OCTAVE BELOW EITHER TWELFTH FRET E.

ALL E'S AS DISCUSSED IN THIS BOOK ARE MUSICALLY EQUAL. NEVERTHELESS DO NOT VOICE ALL THREE ALL THE TIME, OR ALL THREE SIMULTANEOUSLY, IN EVERY E CHORD OR SCALE PLAYED.

The D Chords and Scales

or

"The ②nd / ④th String(s), 1st & 4th Finger(s) Shapes

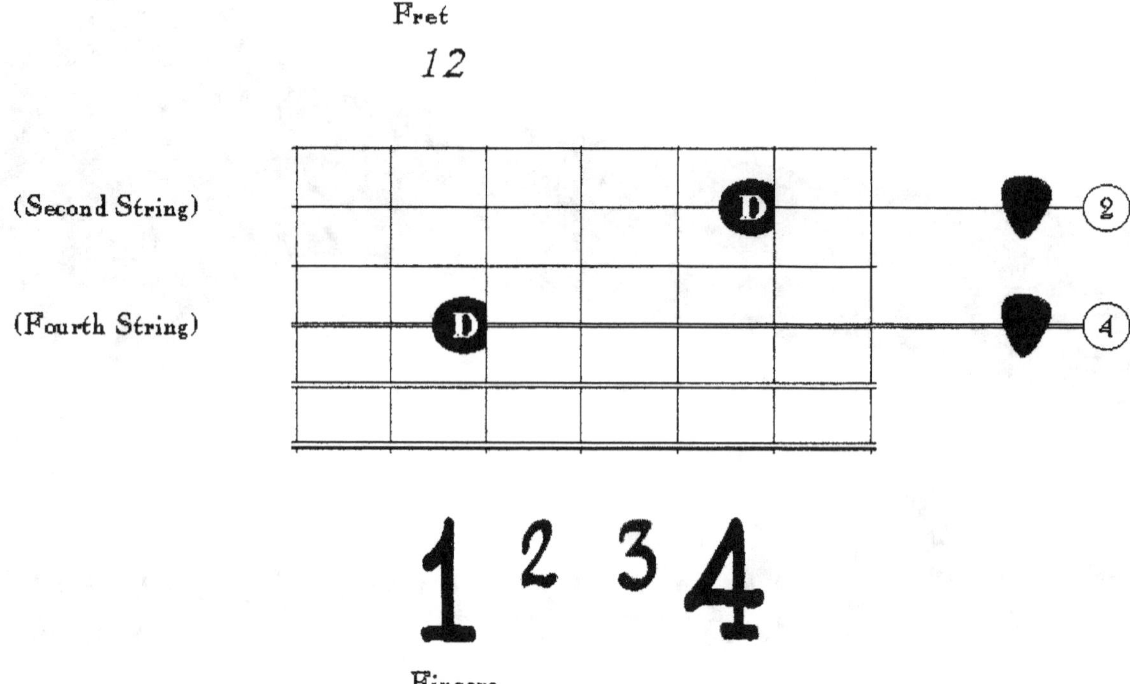

THIS SHAPE CONSTRUCT UNDERSCORES ALL THE D CHORD AND SCALE VOICINGS FOUND IN THIS POSITION. THE MAIN D ROOT NOTE(S) ARE ON THE SECOND / FOURTH STRING(S) AS THE FIRST AND OR FOURTH FINGER(S) DO THE FRETTING. THE JUMBO "DOT(S)" FUNCTION LIKE ANCHOR POINT(S) THAT HELP GROUND THE D FINGER WORK INVOLVED. THAT ASIDE, ONLY A SINGLE D, NOT BOTH, NEEDS TO BE PRESENT IN WHATEVER THE GIVEN D CHORD OR SCALE HAPPENS TO BE. ☞

SOME OF THE D CHORD VOICINGS ASSOCIATED WITH THE GUITAR'S TWELFTH POSITION ARE:

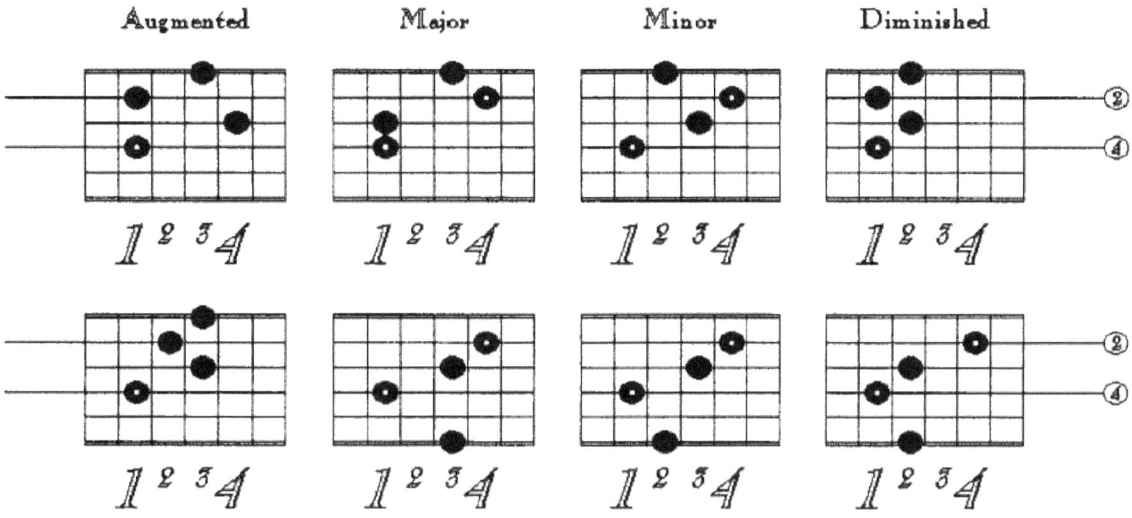

SOME OF THE D SCALE VOICINGS ASSOCIATED WITH THE GUITAR'S TWELFTH POSITION ARE:

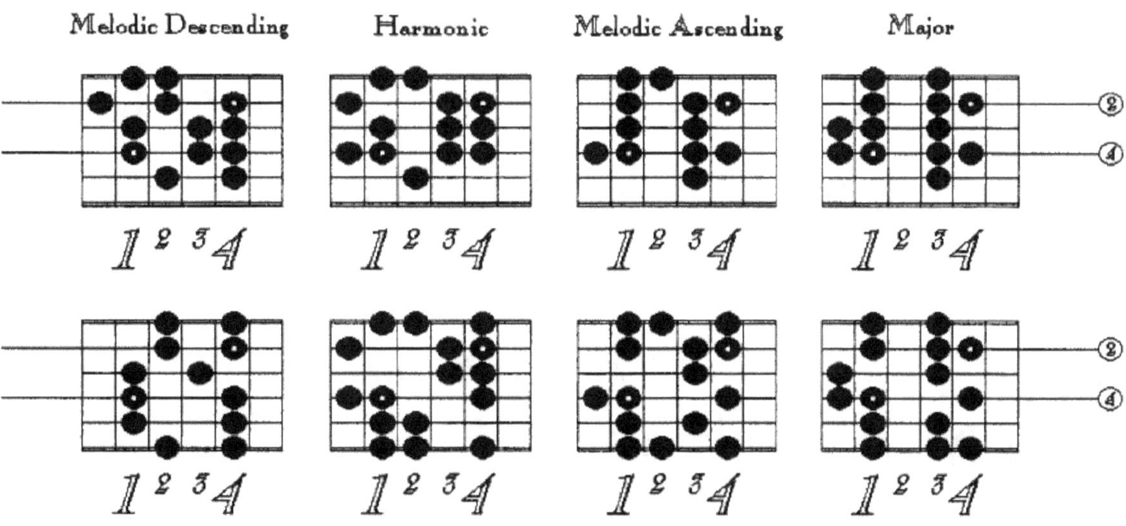

Further Commentary...

As evidenced in the grids on the previous page, all D chords and scales situate themselves in the twelfth position nicely, plus any assorted forms and patterns likewise derived will sound great in any other position too; mind the small adjustment in fingering. The **main** D root note pair is outside what is more often than not the second and third finger realm, and due to this, a fresh sense of technical feel is now brought to the fretting hand. Moreover, recognize that the first finger functions like a capo of sorts a good deal of the time, as it's common for the finger to barre a nearby string. Now contrast that with the fourth finger's circumstances, it basically hammering on or pulling off the notes that it can, or fretting them as desired. Plus,

The **MAIN** D root note on the fourth string is a perfect octave away from the **MAIN** D root note on the second, which is an excellent situation for the fretting hand here to find itself. It's odd that the finger stretching feels innate or to one's liking, this due to the location of the D root note(s). Last, utilize the open strings, the open fourth D making for a shining example. It's one octave away from the **MAIN** D root note on the same string, a pleasant circumstance of which guitarists are sue to exploit.

The **MAIN** D root note(s) discussed in this book are musically equal, but don't voice both every time in every D chord or scale played.

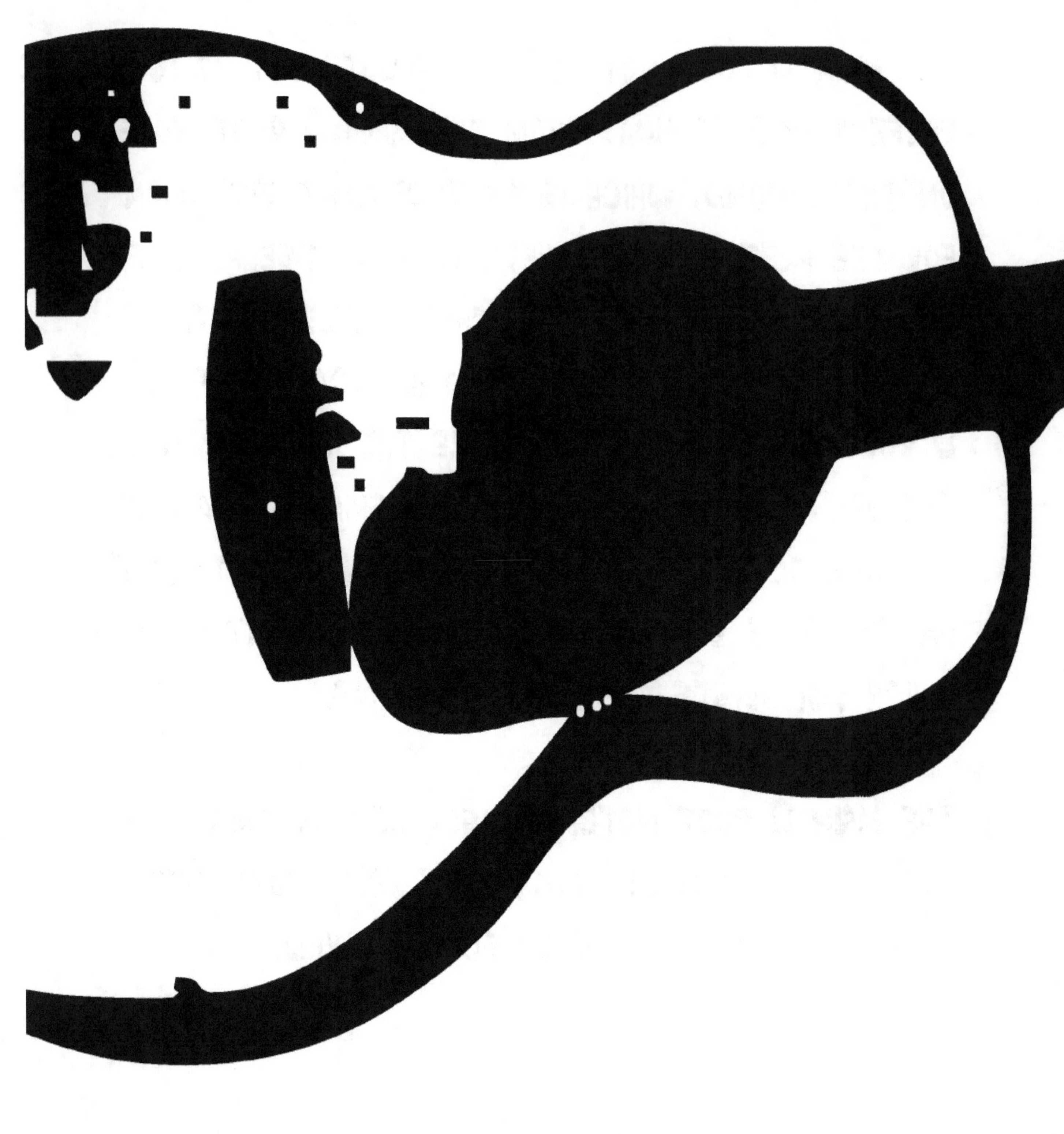

Alphabetical Appendix

Fret

12

(Third String) A A ③

1 2 3 4

Fingers

THE A CHORDS AND SCALES

OR

"THE ③RD STRING, 3RD FINGER SHAPES"

③rd, 3rd - A Chords

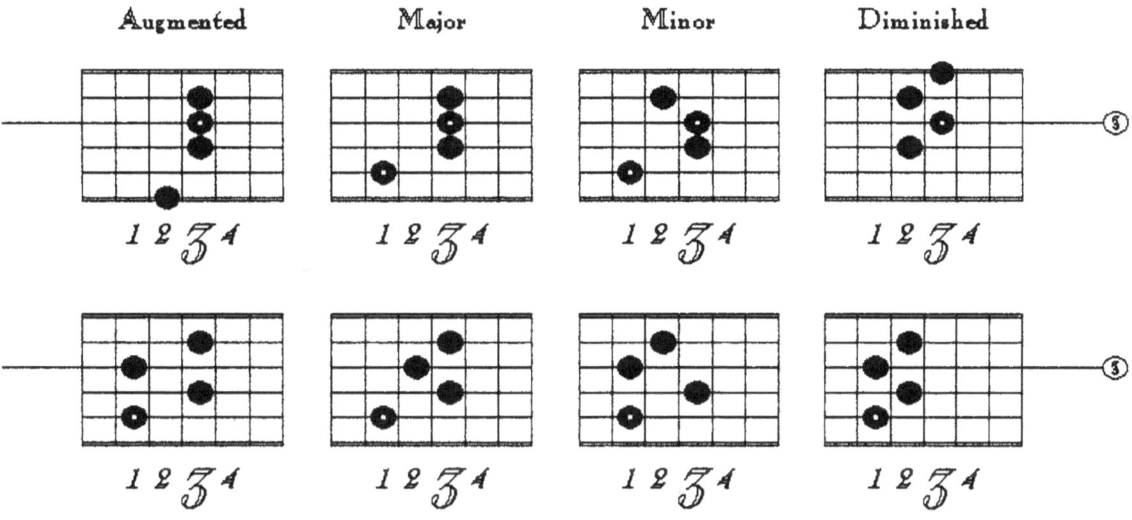

③rd, 3rd - A Scales

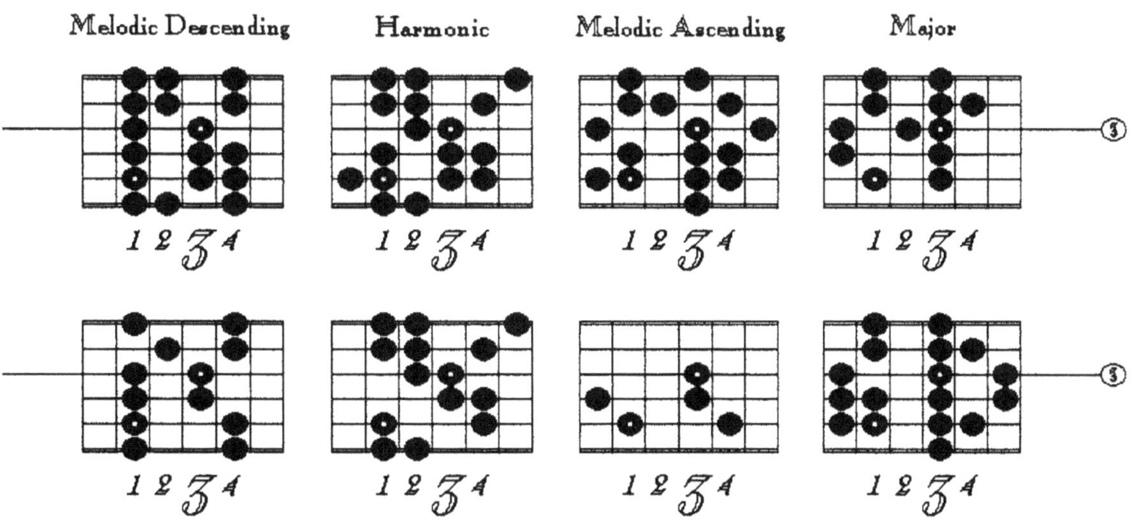

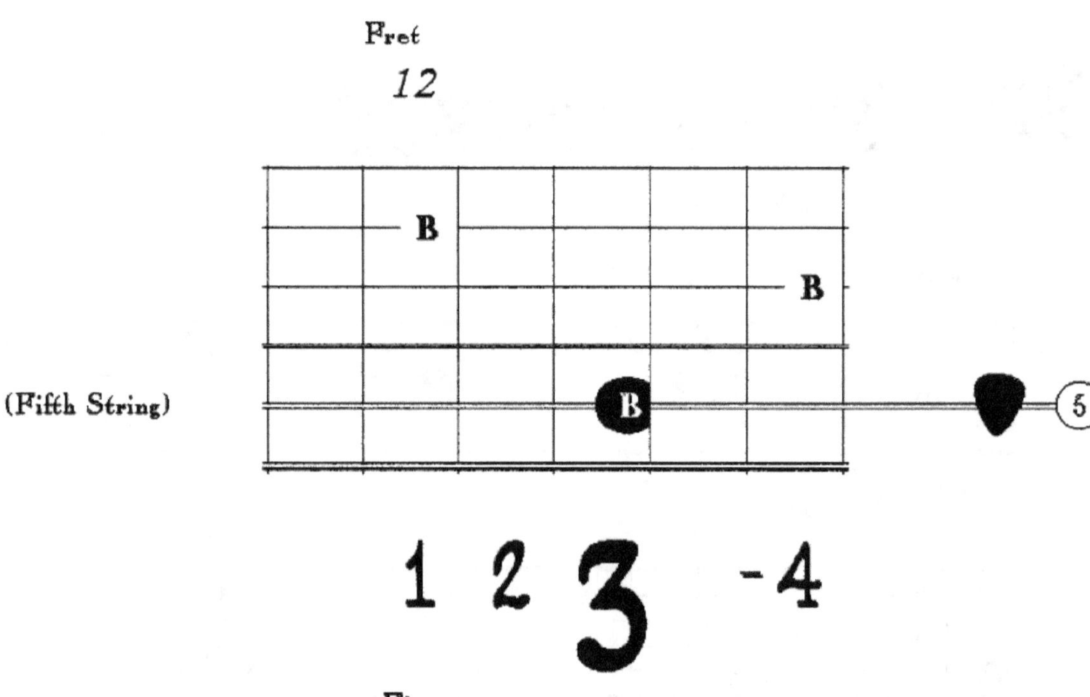

The B Chords and Scales

or

"The ⑤th String, 3rd Finger Shapes"

⑤TH, 3RD -B CHORDS

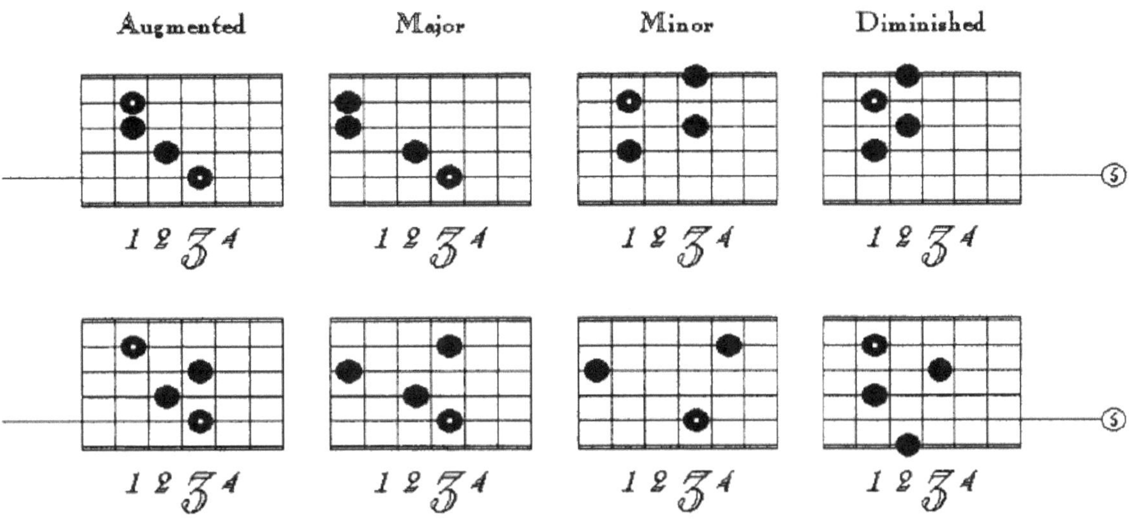

⑤TH, 3RD -B SCALES

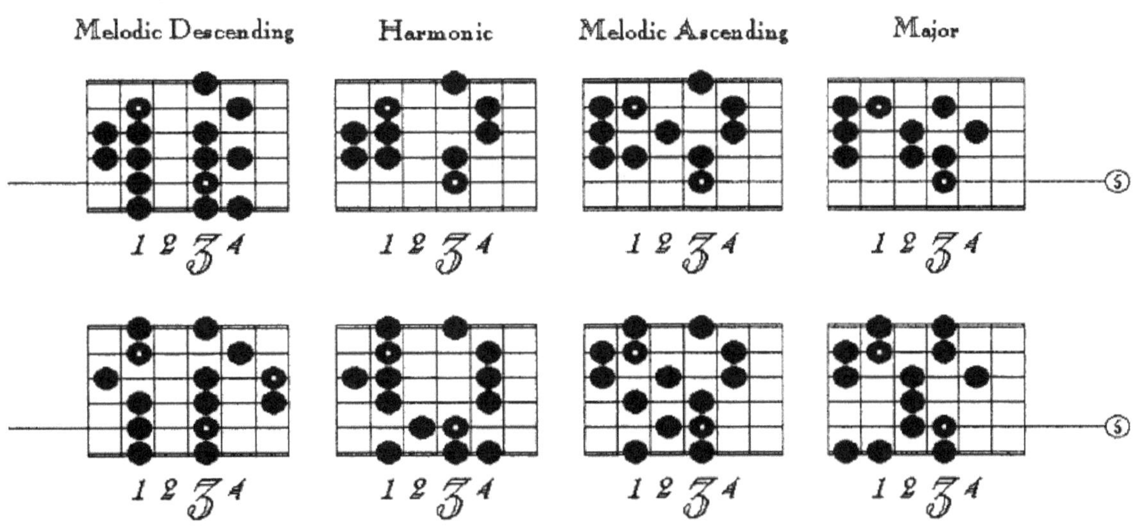

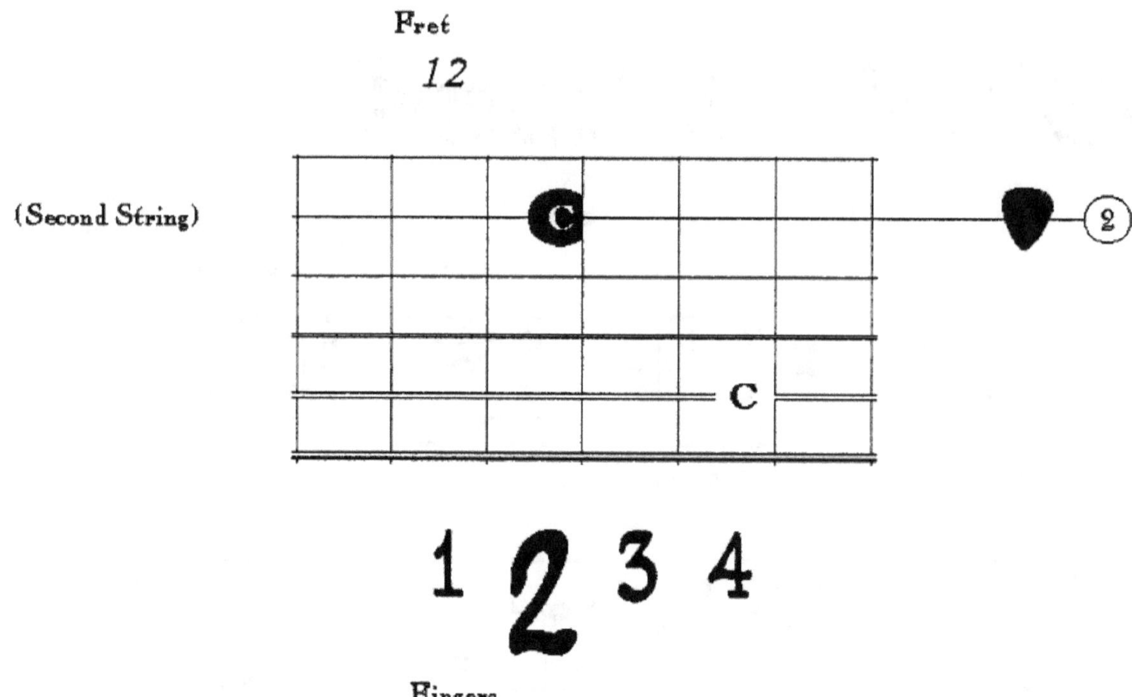

THE C CHORDS AND SCALES

OR

"THE ②ND STRING, 2ND FINGER SHAPES"

②ND, 2ND - C CHORDS

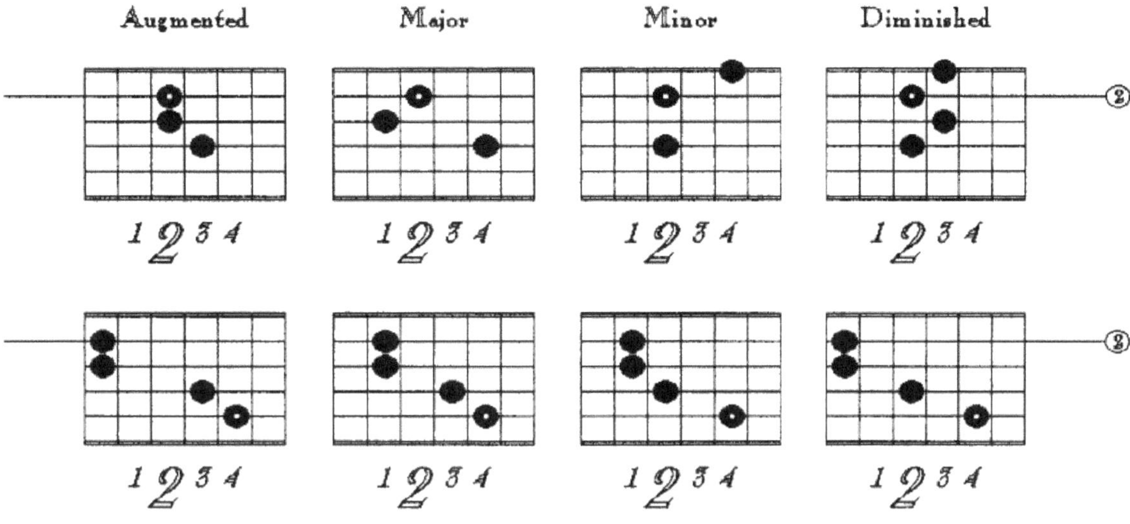

②ND, 2ND - C SCALES

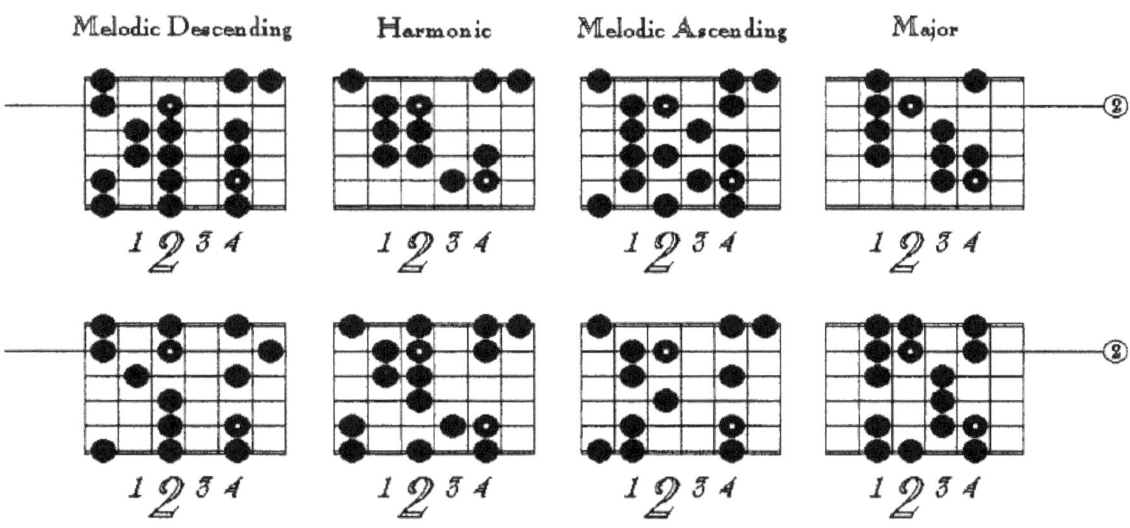

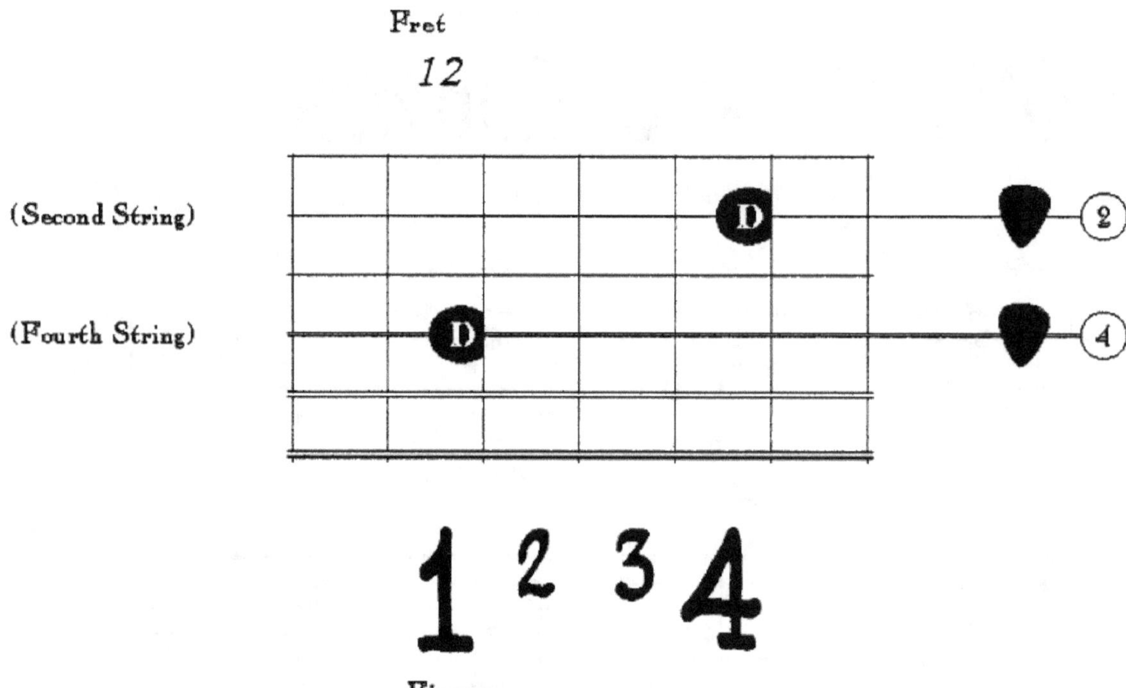

THE D CHORDS AND SCALES

OR

"THE ②ND / ④TH STRING(S), 1ST & 4TH FINGER(S) SHAPES"

②ND ④TH, 1ST & 4TH -D CHORDS

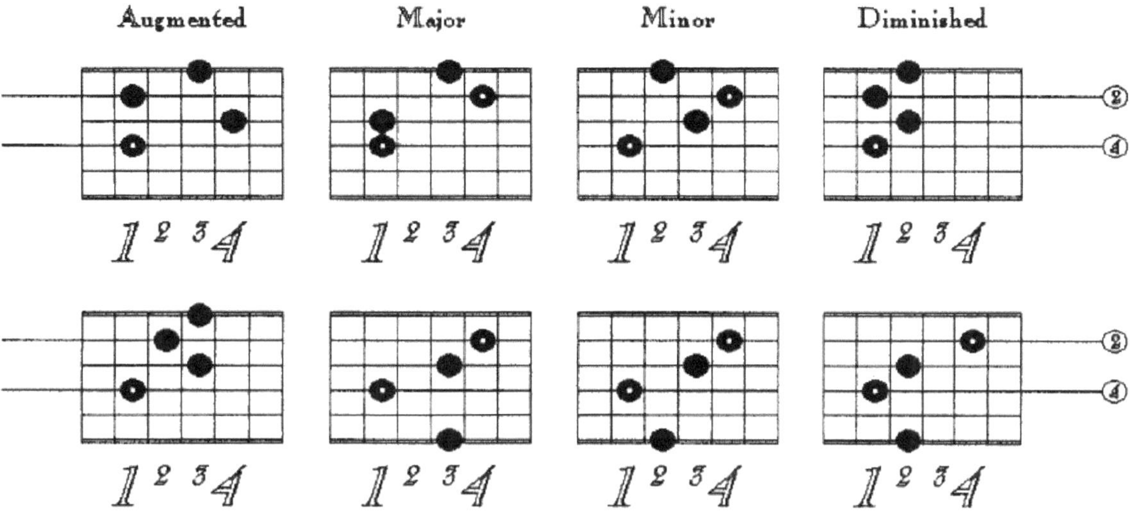

②ND ④TH, 1ST & 4TH -D SCALES

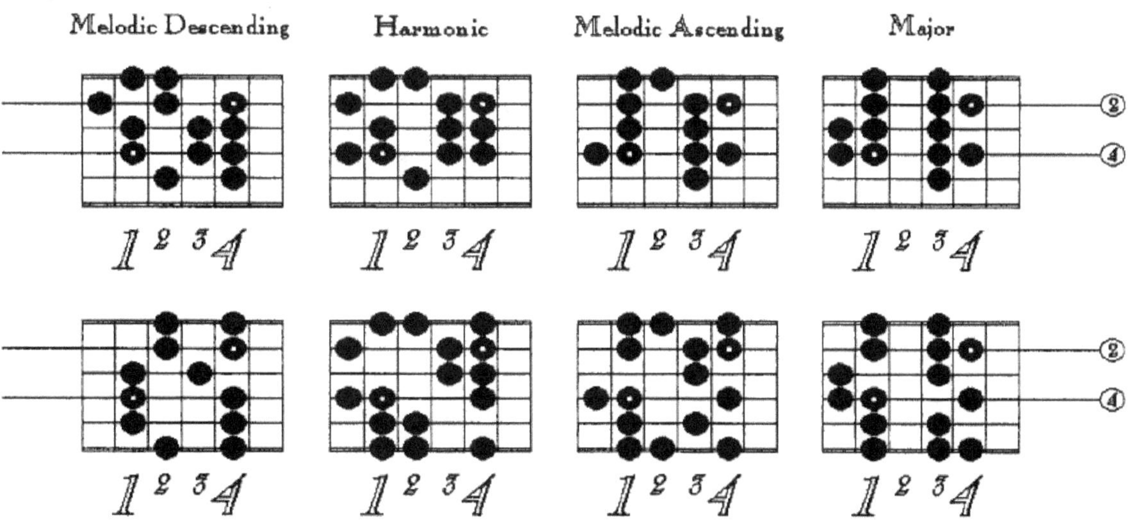

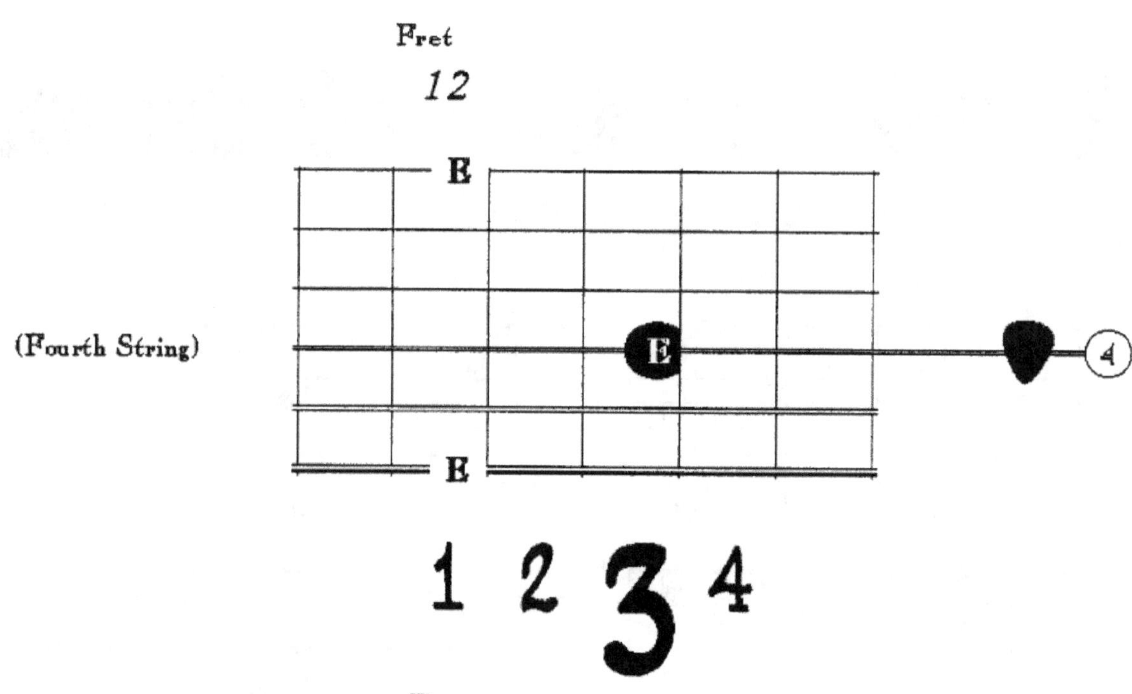

THE E CHORDS AND SCALES

OR

"THE ④TH STRING, 3RD FINGER SHAPES"

④TH, 3RD - E CHORDS

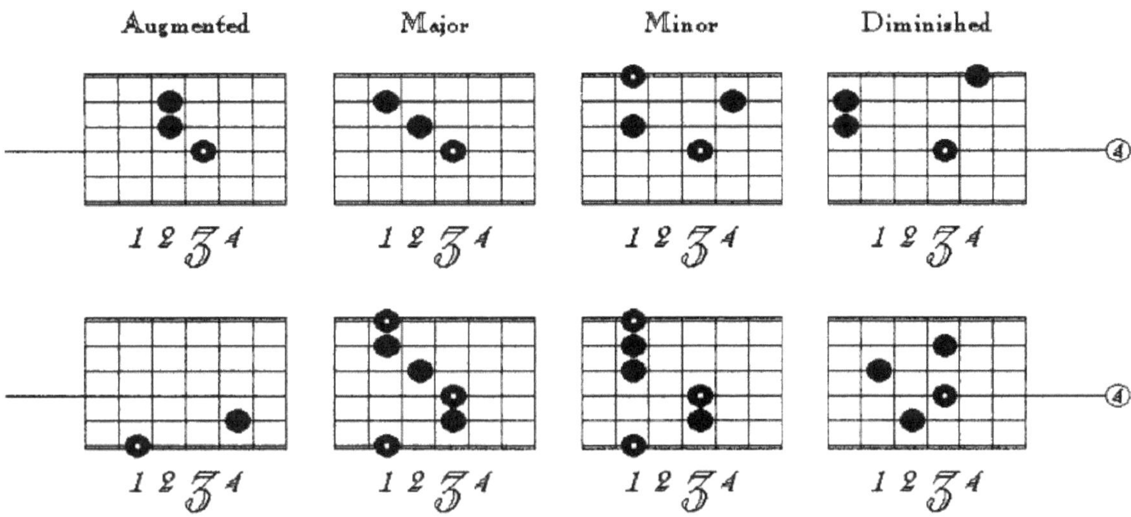

④TH, 3RD - E SCALES

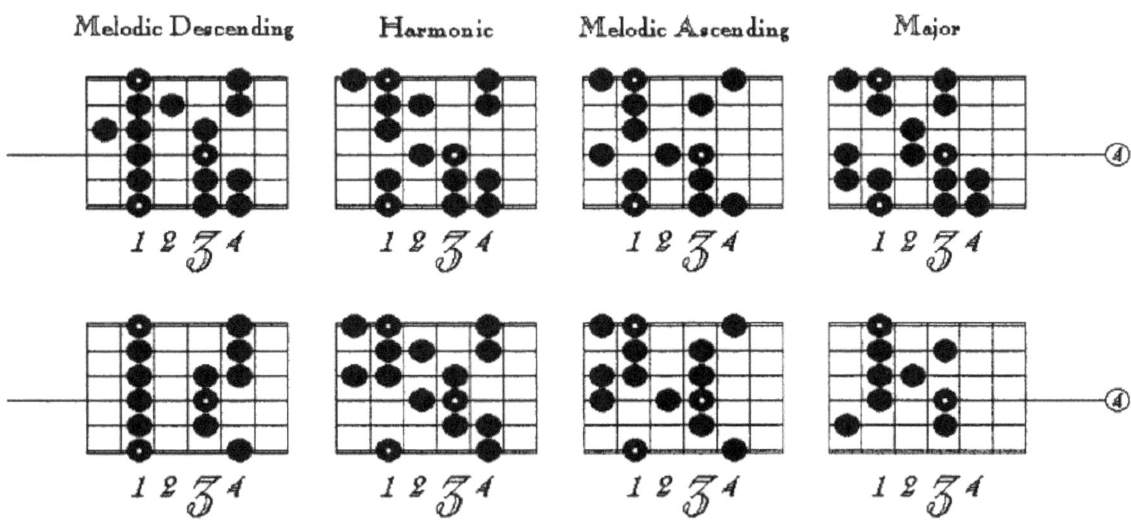

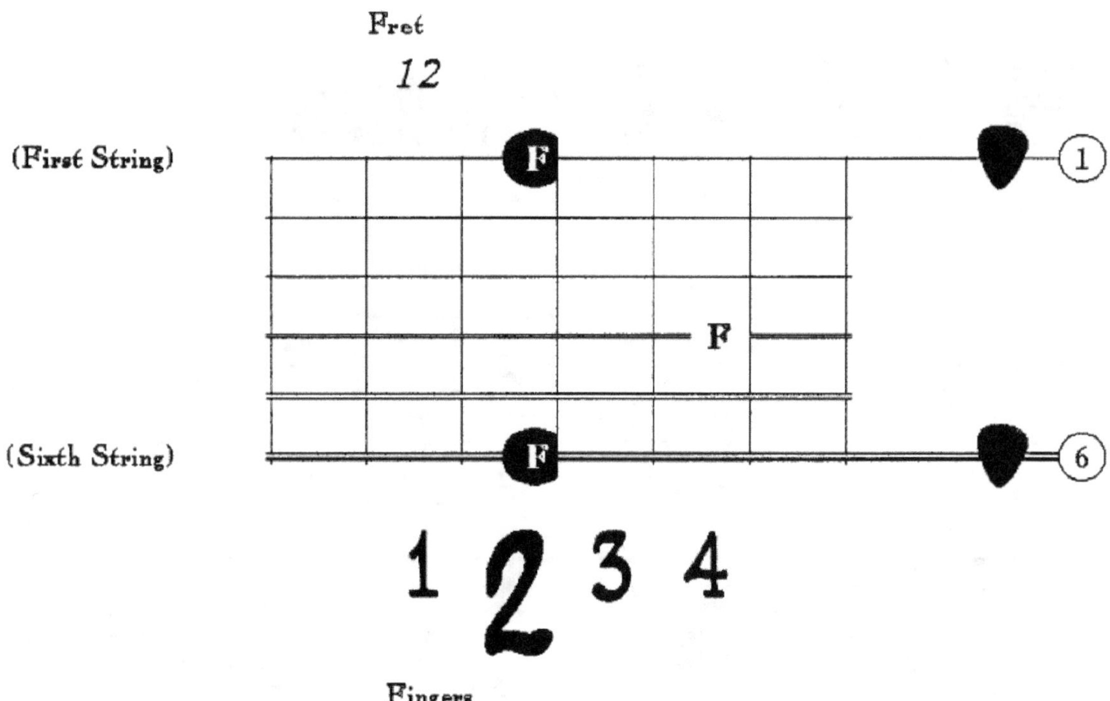

THE F CHORDS AND SCALES

OR

"THE ①ST / ⑥TH STRING(S), 2ND FINGER SHAPES"

①st ⑥th, 2nd - F Chords

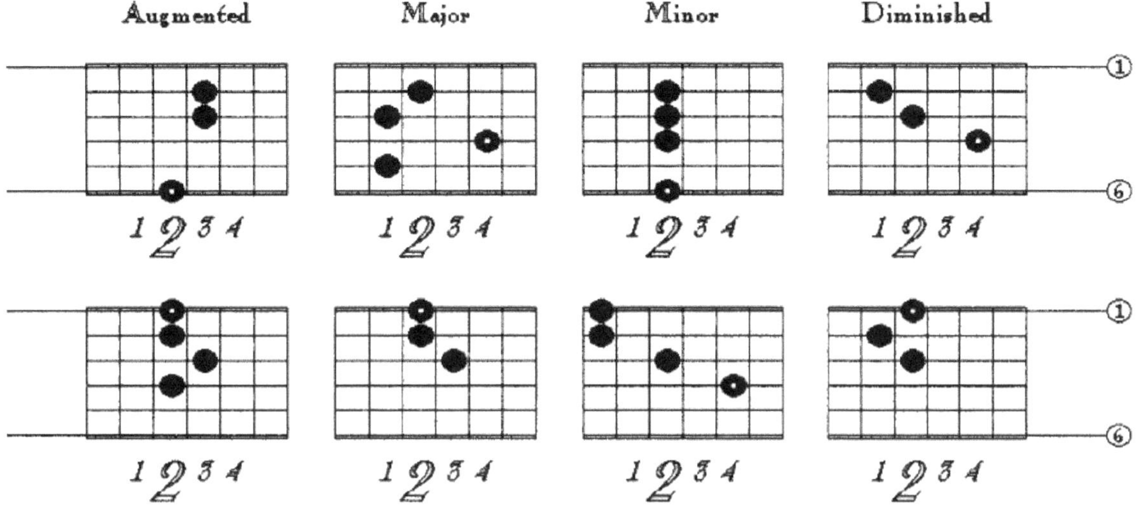

①st ⑥th, 2nd - F Scales

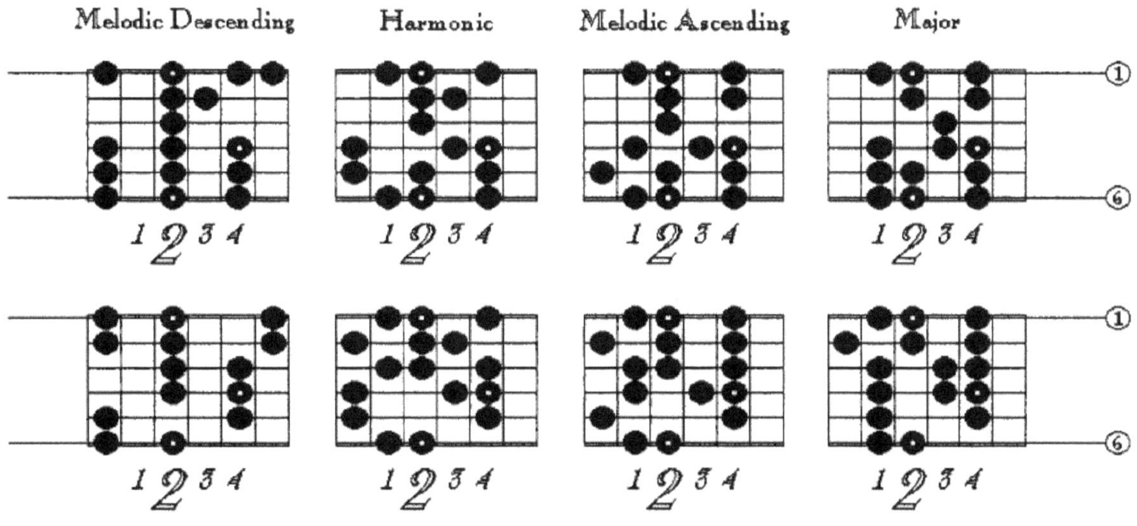

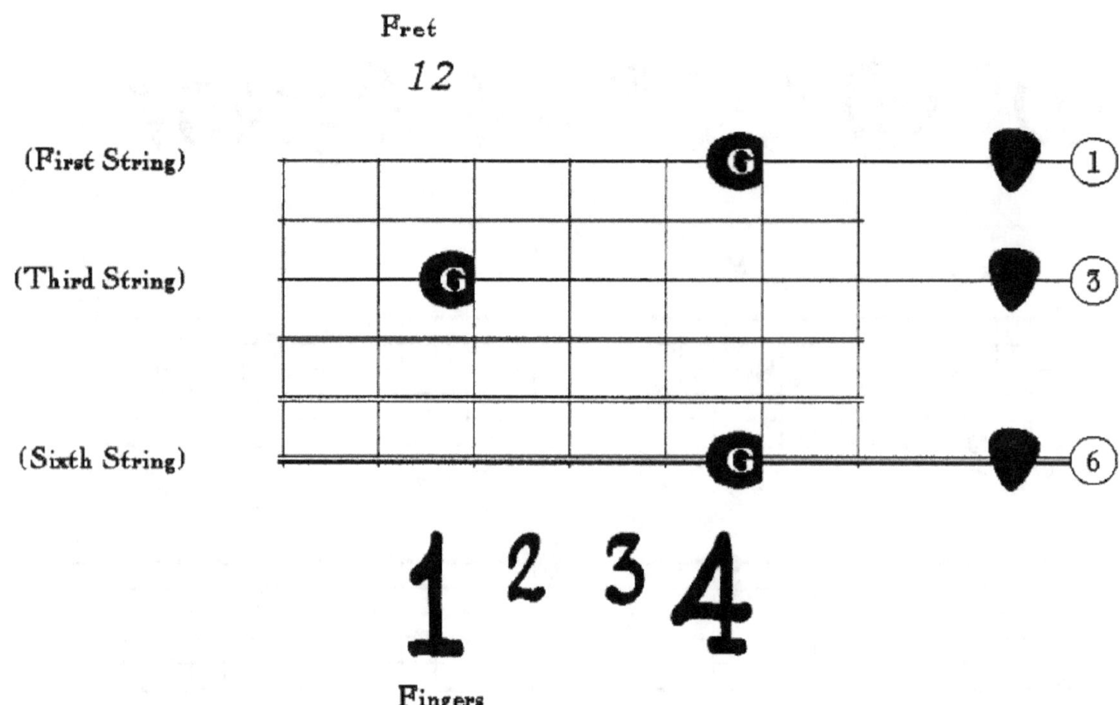

The G Chords and Scales

or

"The ① st / ③ rd / ⑥ th String(s), 1st & 4th Finger(s) Shapes"

①st ③rd ⑥th, 1st & 4th - G Chords

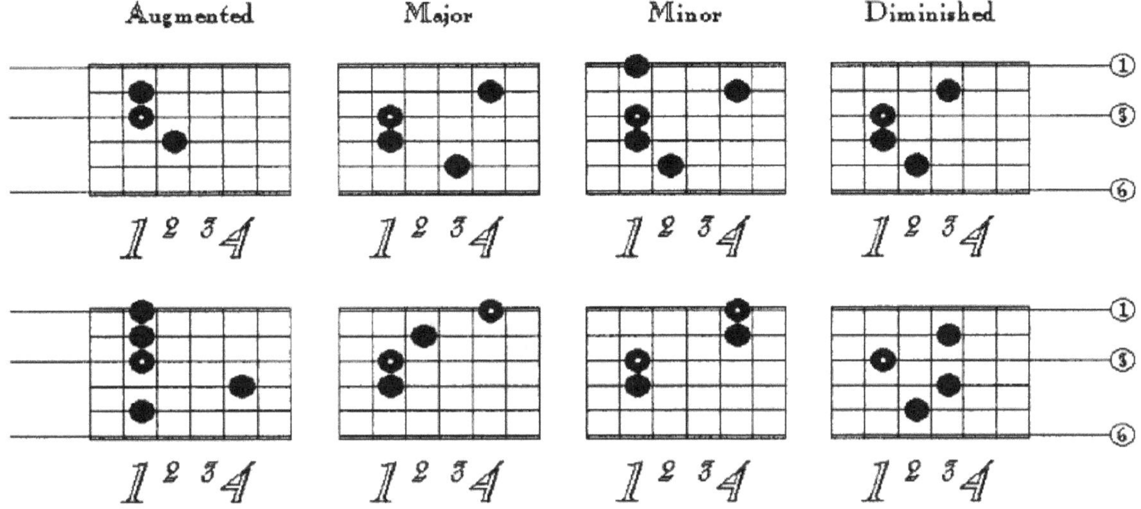

①st ③rd ⑥th, 1st & 4th - G Scales

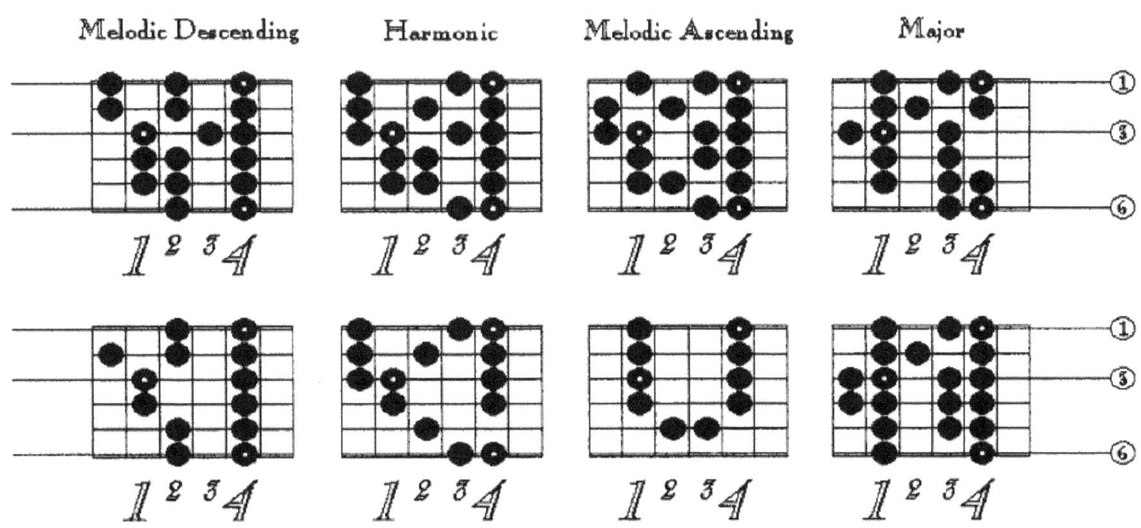

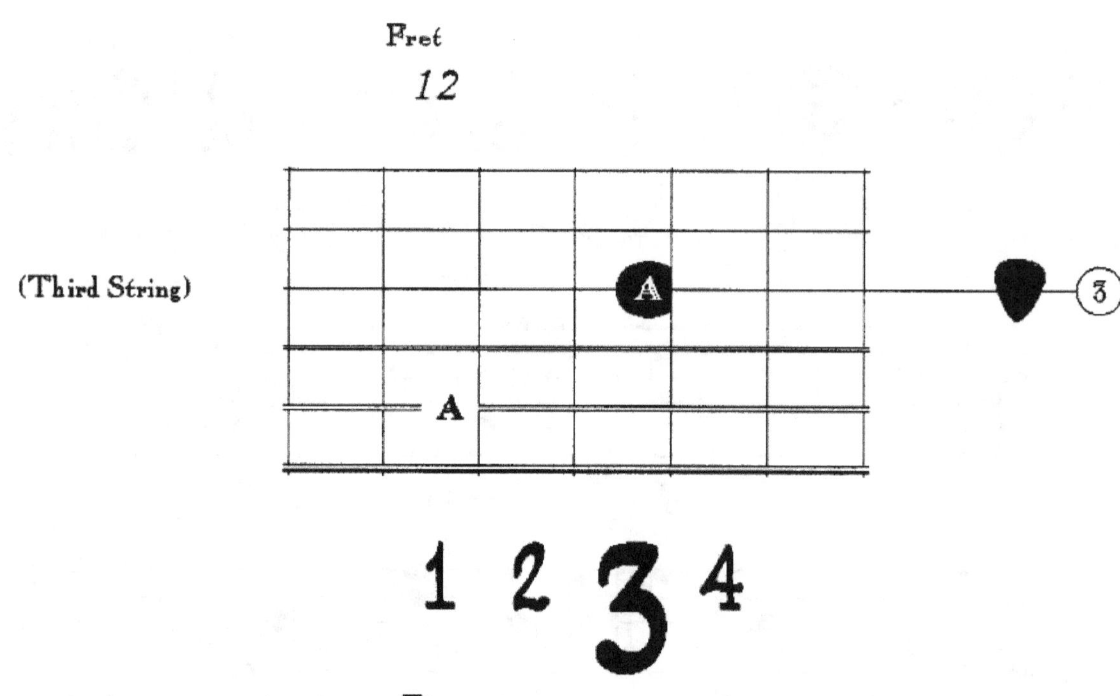

THE A CHORDS AND SCALES

OR

"THE ③RD STRING, 3RD FINGER SHAPES"

③RD, 3RD - A CHORDS

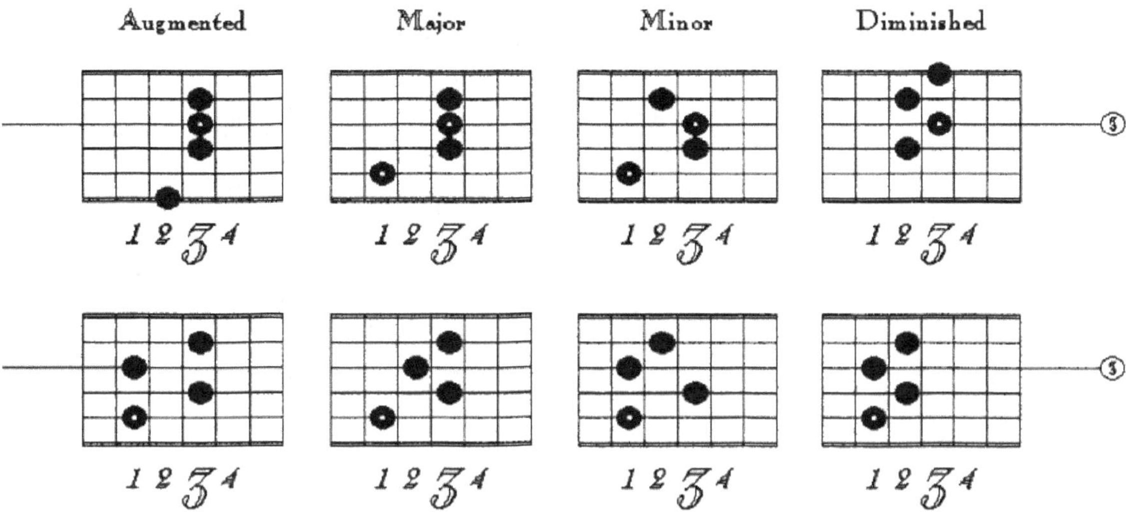

③RD, 3RD - A SCALES

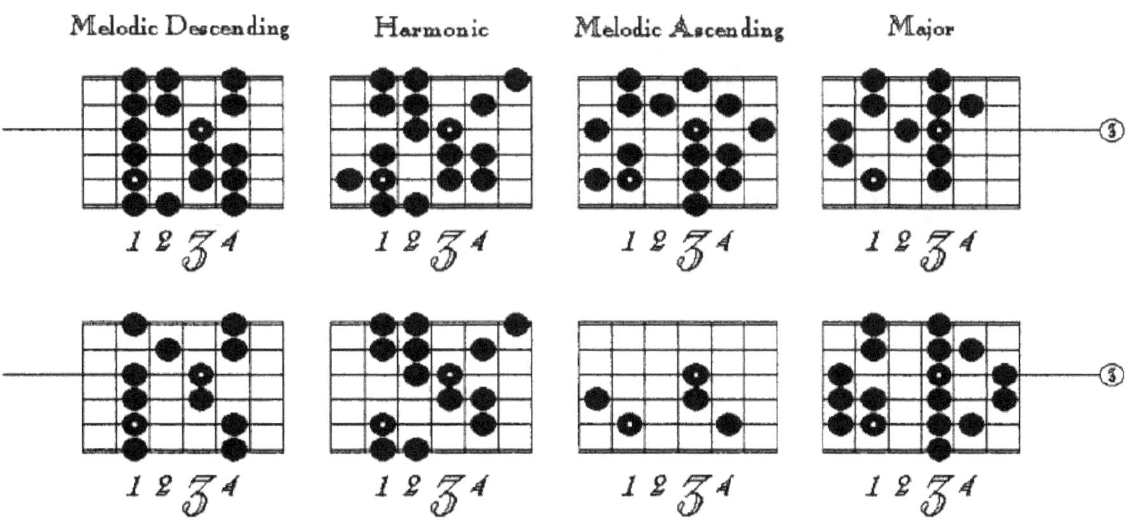

Notation & Tablature

www.ingramcontent.com/pod-product-compliance
Lightning Source LLC
LaVergne TN
LVHW061247100826
845148LV00008B/1055

* 9 7 8 0 5 7 8 8 2 5 6 4 9 *